The Mishkat Al-Anwar of Al-Ghazzali

By

Al-Ghazali

First published in 1924

Published by Left of Brain Books

Copyright © 2023 Left of Brain Books

ISBN 978-1-396-32652-3

First Edition

All rights reserved. No part of this publication may be reproduced, distributed, or transmitted in any form or by any means, including photocopying, recording, or other electronic or mechanical methods, without the prior written permission of the publisher, except in the case of brief quotations permitted by copyright law. Left of Brain Books is a division of Left Of Brain Onboarding Pty Ltd.

PUBLISHER'S PREFACE

About the Book

The Mishkat Al-Anwar (The Niche for Lights) by Al-Ghazzali, translated by W.H.T. Gairdner.

About the Author

Al-Ghazali (1058 - 1111)

"Abu Hamed Mohammad ibn Mohammad al-Ghazzali (1058-1111), known as Algazel to the western medieval world, born and died in Tus, in the Khorasan province of Persia (modern day Iran). He was a Muslim theologian, jurist, philosopher, and mystic of Persian origin and remains one of the most celebrated scholars in the history of Sufi Islamic thought. Moreover, one of his major works, The Incoherence of the Philosophers, changed the course of Islamic thought, shifting it away from the influence of ancient Greek and Hellenistic philosophy, and towards cause-and-effect that were determined by Allah or intermediate"

(Quote from wikipedia.org)

CONTENTS

PUBLISHER'S PREFACE
ACKNOWLEDGMENT 1
AUTHOR'S PREFACE 2
INTRODUCTION 4
    DATE, OBJECT, AND GENERAL CONTENTS.................................... 5
    MYSTERIES LEFT VEILED IN THIS TREATISE 7
    A GHAZZALIAN PHILOSOPHY OF RELIGION 9
    GHAZZALI PROBLEMS RAISED BY THE FOREGOING 15
    THE PROBLEM OF THE VICEGERENT IN IBN RUSHD AND IBN TUFAIL 18
    ONE SOLUTION OF THE PROBLEM OF THE VICEGERENT 23
    ANOTHER SOLUTION 29
    AL-GHAZZALI AND THE SEVEN SPHERES 38
    ANTHROPOMORPHISM AND THEOMORPHISM IN AL-MISHKAT 42
    PANTHEISM AND AL-GHAZZALI, IN AL-MISHKAT 50
    TRANSLATION 58
    PART I.--LIGHT, AND LIGHTS: PRELIMINARY STUDIES 62
    PART II.--THE SCIENCE OF SYMBOLISM 88
    PART III.--THE APPLICATION TO THE LIGHT-VERSE AND THE VEILS TRADITION 106

ACKNOWLEDGMENT

I HAVE greatly profited from hints, generously lavished in the course of correspondence, from Professors D.B. MACDONALD, R. NICHOLSON, and LOUIS MASSIGNON, in addition to recent works by the last two. My cordial thanks to these; and also to Professor D.S. MARGOLIOUTH for discussing with me some of the difficult points in the translation.

AUTHOR'S PREFACE

I AM so conscious that my general equipment was insufficient to warrant my having undertaken an introduction to this treatise (in addition to the translation), that my utmost hope is this,--that what I have written may be regarded by lenient Orientalists as something to elicit--provoke, if you will--the necessary supplementing and formative criticism; or as useful materials to be built into some more authoritative and better informed work: and that they may from this point of view be inclined to pardon what otherwise might seem an unwarrantable piece of rashness and indiscretion.

A still greater presumption remains to be forgiven, but this time on the ground of the great human simplicities, when I venture to inscribe this work, in spite of everything, to the beloved memory of

IGNAZ GOWZIHER

--that golden-hearted man--who in 1911 introduced me to the Mishkât; and to join with his name that of who first introduced me to the Mishkât's author. Of these twain, the latter may perhaps forgive the lapses of a pupil because of the filial joy with which, I know well, he will see the two names joined together, howsoever or by whomsoever it was done. As for the former, . . . in Abraham's bosom all things are forgiven.

DUNCAN BLACK MACDONALD

CAIRO

July, 1923.

INTRODUCTION

THE references in square brackets are to the pages of the Cairo Arabic edition, and to the present English translation.

THE MISHKÂT AL-ANWAR [1] is a work of extreme interest from the viewpoint of al-Ghazzâlî's [2] inner life and esoteric thought. The glimpses it gives of that life and thought are remarkably, perhaps uniquely, intimate. It begins where his autobiographical Al-Munqidh min al-Dalâl leaves off. Its esotericism excited the curiosity and even the suspicion of Muslim thinkers from the first, and we have deeply interesting allusions to it in Ibn Tufaill [3] and Ibn Rushd] [4] the celebrated philosophers of Western Islam, who flourished within the century after al-Ghazzâlî's death in 1111 (A.H. 505)--a fact which, again, increases its importance and interest for us.

---

[1] The Mishkât al-Anwâr is numbered No. 34 in Brockelmann's Geschichte der Arabischen Literatur (vol. i, p. 423). It was printed in Cairo (matba`at as Sidq, A. H. 1322), to which edition the references in the present work are made. There is another edition in a collection of five opuscules of Ghazzâlî under the title of the first of the five, Faisal al-Tafriqa.

[2] The Algazal of the Schoolmen.

[3] The Abubacer of the Schoolmen

[4] The Averroes of the Schoolmen

DATE, OBJECT, AND GENERAL CONTENTS

THERE is no way of fixing the Precise date of this treatise; but it falls among his later ones, perhaps among the latest; the most important hint we get from Ghazzâlî himself being that the book was written after his Magnum opus, the Ihyâ'al Ulûm (p. [9]). Other works of Ghazzâlî mentioned by him in this treatise are the Mi`âr al-`Ilm, Mahakk al-Nazar, and al-Maqsad al-Asnâ.

The object of the opuscule is to expound a certain Koran verse and a certain Tradition. The former is the celebrated Light-Verse (S. 24, 35) and the latter the Veils-Tradition. It is divided into three sections, of which the first is considerably the longest.

In this first section he considers the word "light" itself, and its plural "lights," as applied to physical light and lights; to the eye; to the intelligence (i.e. intellect or reason); to prophets; to supernal beings; and finally to Allah himself, who is shown to be not the only source of light and of these lights, but also the only real actual light in all existence. In the second section we have some most interesting prolegomena to the whole subject of symbolic language in the Koran and Traditions, and its interpretation. Symbols are shown to be no mere metaphors. There is a real mystical nexus between symbol and symbolized, type and antitype, outer and inner. The symbols are infinitely numerous, very much more numerous than those mentioned in Koran, or Traditions. Every object on earth "perhaps" has its correlative in the unseen, spiritual world. This doctrine of symbols reminds us of the Platonic "ideas" and their earthly copies, and of the "patterns of things in the heavens" and "the example and shadow [on earth] of heavenly things" in the Epistle to the Hebrews. A notable deduction is made from this doctrine, namely, the equal incumbency of keeping the outward letter (zâhir) of the Law as well as its inner meaning (bâṯin). Nearly all the most advanced Ṣûfis were zealous and Minutely scrupulous keepers of the ritual, ceremonial, and other prescriptions of the Sunna law, and Ghazzâlî here supplies a quasi-philosophical basis for this fidelity--a fidelity which some of the bolder and more extreme mystics found illogical and "unspiritual".

In the third section the results of this symbology are applied to the Verse and Tradition in question. In the former the beautiful, and undeniably intriguing expressions of the Koran--the Light, the Niche, the Glass, the Oil, Tree, the East and the West--are explained both on psychological and religio-metaphysical lines; and a similar exegesis is applied to the tradition of the Seventy Thousand Veils.

MYSTERIES LEFT VEILED IN THIS TREATISE

IN the course of all this Ghazzâlî gives us, incidentally, much that excites our curiosity to the highest degree; though always, when we get to the crucial point, we meet a "perhaps," or a patronizing allusion to the immaturity of his less-initiated reader. (Ghazzâlî's hesitations--"it may be," "perhaps", etc.--are worthy of study in this treatise. They do not so much have the impression of hesitancy in his own mind, as of a desire to "fence" a little with his reader.) He himself writes "incommunicable mystery"' across a number of these passages. Thus, the nature of the human intelligence and its peculiar affinity to the divine (pp. 16, 71); the mystic "state" of al-Hallâj, and other "inebriates," and the expressions they emit in their mystic intoxication (p. [20]) --"behind which truths," says Ghazzâlî, "also lie secrets which it is not lawful to enter upon"; the astounding passage (p. [24]) in which to the supreme Adept of the mystical Union with deity are ascribed features and functions of very deity; the real explanation of the word tawhîd, involving as it does the question of the reality of the universe and the nature of the soul's union or identification with deity; the nature of the Commander (al-Mutâ`) of the universe, and whether he be Allah or an ineffable supreme Vicegerent; who that Vicegerent is, and why it must be he and not Allâh who performs the prime function of the cosmos-ruler, viz. the issue of the command for the moving of the primum mobile, whereby all the motions of the Heavenly (and the Sublunary) spheres are set a-going; and the final mystery of Allah-an-sich, a Noumenal Deity, in whose case transcendence is to be carried to such a pitch that gnosticism and agnosticism meet, and the validity of every possible or conceivable predication is denied, whether of act or attribute (see p. [55])--all these things are incommunicable mysteries, secrets, from the revealing of which our author turns away at the exact moment when we expect the denouement. The art is supreme--but something more than tantalizing. Who were the adepts to whom he did communicate these thrilling secrets? Were these communications ever written down for or by his brother initiates? Or did he ever communicate them? Was there really anything to communicate? If so, what?

A GHAZZALIAN PHILOSOPHY OF RELIGION

ON the whole it is the final section on the Veils-Tradition which, though really of the nature of an appendix, contains the most numerous and the most interesting problems for the study of Ghazâlî's inner life, thought, and convictions. This tradition speaks of "Seventy Thousand Veils of Light and Darkness" which veil pure Godhead from the human soul. The origin of the tradition is, it is safe to hazard, Neoplatonic, and it therefore lent itself completely to the gnostic and theosophical mode of thought which so soon invaded Muslim Sûfism after its less successful effort to capture orthodox Christianity. Accordingly Muslim mystics seem to have seized upon the tradition with avidity, though they interpret it variously. For an entirely Neoplatonic, theosophical interpretation, as expounded by Rifâ`i dervishes, the translator's "'Way' of a Mohammedan Mystic" may be consulted. [1] According to this version, the soul, in its upward Seven-fold Way to Union with pure Deity, is at every stage stripped of 10,000 of these Veils, the dark ones first and then the bright. After that the naked soul stands face to face with naked Deity, with Absolute Being, with an unveiled Sun, with unadulterated Light. Ghazâlî's treatment is different. According to him, these Veils are various according to the varieties of the natures which they veil from the One Real. And it is the classification of these natures, which is thus involved, that supplies rich material for an unusually inside view of Ghazâlî's real views concerning men, doctrines, religions, and sects. It is not the orthodox schoolman, the fierce dogmat-

---

[1] The Moslem World, year 1912, pp. 171 seqq., 245 seqq.; as separatum, Otto Harrassowitz, pp. 9, 10

ist, the rigid mutakallim, who is now speaking. We have the sensation of overhearing Ghazzâlî as he speaks aloud to his own soul, or to a circle of initiates. It is hardly less than an outline of a philosophy of religion with which we have to do. He divides mankind into four classes: those veiled with veils of pure darkness; those veiled with veils of mixed darkness and light; those veiled with veils of pure light; and those who attain to the vision of the Unveiled. Every line of this part of the work merits and requires the closest study. It is not possible to give this detailed study here--it has been given elsewhere, and to that the reader must be referred.[1] But a summary of Ghazzâlî's classification of souls and creeds may be given here, for thus, even more effectively than by an extended study, may a vivid preliminary appreciation be gained of the importance of this section for students of the Ghazzâlî problem. He begins at the bottom and works up the light-ladder, rung by rung, to the very top, thus giving a gradation of human natures and human creeds in respect of their approach to absolute truth. Sometimes the grades are definitely identified by the author. In other cases they may be certainly, or nearly certainly, identified from the description he gives. In the following summary Ghazzâlî's own identifications are given between round brackets; inferred identifications certain or nearly certain, between square brackets.

Class I.--Those veiled with Veils of pure Darkness

Atheists--

(a) Naturist philosophers whose god is Nature,

(b) Egotists whose god is Self.

---

[1] Der Islam, year 1914, in Nos. 2 and 3: by the present writer

Subdivisions of (b):--

(1) Seekers after sensual pleasures (the bestial attributes).

(2) Seekers after dominion ("Arabs, some Kurds, and (the very numerous Fools").

(3) Seekers after filthy lucre

(4) Seekers after vainglory

(2-4) (the ferocious attributes).

Class II.--Those veiled with Veils of mixed Darkness and Light

A. THOSE WHOSE DARKNESS ORIGINATES IN THE SENSES

(1) Image-worshippers. [Polytheists of the Hellenic (? and Indian) type.]

(2) Worshippers of animate objects of physical beauty. (Some of the most remote Turkish tribes.)

(3) Fire-worshippers. [Magians.]

(4) Astrologizing Star-worshippers. [Star-worshippers of Ḥarran: ?Ṣabîans.]

(5) Sun-worshippers.

(6) Light-worshippers, with their dualistic acknowledgement of a supreme correlative Darkness. (Zoroastrians of the cult of Ormuzd and Ahrimân.)

B. THOSE WHOSE DARKNESS ORIGINATES IN THE IMAGINATION

(who worship a One Being, sitting [spatially] on his throne).

(1) Corporealists. {p. 11}

[Extreme Ḥanbalites: Ẓâhirites.]

(2) Karrâmites.

(3) Those who have eliminated all spatial ideas in regard to Allâh except the literal "up-above".

[Ibn Ḥanbal.[1] Ḥanbalites.[2]]

C. THOSE WHOSE DARKNESS ORIGINATES IN THE [DISCURSIVE] INTELLIGENCE[3]

[Various sorts of Mutakallimîn]

(1) Anthropomorphists in respect of the Seven Attributes of Allah, "Hearing, Seeing," etc., and especially the "Word" of Allah.

---

[1] Faisal al-Tafriqa, p. 10.

[2] Averroes adds to these (with justice) the Koran; Mohammed himself; the "Early Fathers"; al-Ash'ari; and the early Ash`arites--before the time of Abul Ma'âli," says Averroes, loc. cit. i.e. of al-Juwainî, The Imâm al-Haramain, our author's Shaikh, d. 478 (see his al-Kashf 'an manâhij al-adillâ', ed. Müller, p. 65, Cairo ed., p. 54.

[3] For according to Ghazzâlî the genuine axiomata of the pure intelligence are infallible. See p. [10], and an important autobiographical passage near the beginning of the Munqidh.]

(Those who said that the Word of Allah has letters and sounds like ours.) [Early literalists; Hanbalites: early Ash`arites.]

(2) Those who said that the word of Allah is like our mental speech (hadith al-nafs.)

[Later Ash`arites.]

Class III.--Those veiled by pure Light

[i.e. purged of all anthropomorphism (tashbîh)]

(1) Those whose views about the Attributes were sound, but who refused to define Allah by means of them: replying to the question "What is the Lord of the World?" by saying, "The Lord, who transcends the ideas of those attributes; He, the Mover and Orderer of the Heavens."

[Hasan al-Basrî, al-Shâfi`î, and others of the bilâ kaifa school.]

(2) Those who mounted higher than the preceding, in declaring that Allah is the mover of only the primum mobile (the Ninth and outermost Heaven), which causes the movement of the other Eight, mediated by their respective Angels.

[Sûfî philosophers. (?) Al-Fârâbî.]

(3) Those who mount higher than these {p. 13} again, in putting a supreme Angel in place of Allah, Who now moves the heavens by commanding this supreme Angel, but not immediately by direct action.

[Sûfî philosophers. Al-Ghazzâlî himself when coram populo (Munqidh, p 11)!]

Class IV.--The Unveiled who Attain

Those who will predicate nothing whatsoever of Allah, and refuse to allow that He even issues the order for the moving of the primum mobile. This Commander (Mutâ`) is now a Vicegerent, who is related to the Absolute Being as the sun to Essential Light or live coal to the Element of Fire.

(1) Adepts who preserve self-consciousness in their absorption in this Absolute, all else being effaced.

(2) Adepts whose self-consciousness is also effaced ("the Fewest of the Few") [al-Hallâj and the extreme Mystics],

(a) who attain to this State with a single leap--as Abraham "al-Khalîl" did, {p. 14}

(b) who attain to it by stages,--as Mohammed "al-Habîb" did [at the Mi`râj].

GHAZZALI PROBLEMS RAISED BY THE FOREGOING

THE mere perusal of this graded scale of systems and of souls shows at once its extraordinary interest because of its revelation of Ghazzâlî's innermost thought about these things, and because of the piquancy and difficulty of some of the problems raised. In the discussion of the whole subject the reader is referred to, the monograph upon the Mishkât to which allusion has been made. The problems may be indicated here in the form of questions, for the sake of defining them as particularly as possible:--

(1) How is it that some reputable Moslems are grouped with Idolators and Dualists in the second division ("mixed light and dark")?

(2) How is it that Jews and Christians are neither mentioned nor alluded to in this rather full sketch for a philosophy of religion? And where could they have been fitted in if they had been mentioned?

(3) How is it that the later Ash`arites, the standard orthodox Theologians, are placed so low, viz. in the division where there are still veils of darkness?

(4) How is that the Mu`tazilites are neither mentioned nor alluded to; and that, according to the differentia of the highest section of the second division, it would be inevitable to place them above the orthodox Ash`arites?

(5) How is it that the most pious believers of the earliest and most venerated type come no higher than the lowest section of the third division?

(6) How is it that to such men is ascribed any special concern about Allah as "mover of the Heavens" [1]

(7) How is it that the various doctrines about the mode of this Moving of the Heavens is made the main if not the sole differentia of the (ascending) grades of this division, though in other works Ghazzâlî treats this very matter with marked coolness [2] How is it that on this is explicitly said to turn the superiority of the schools of Sûfî's over the pious Believers, and the superiority of one school of Sûfî's over another?

(8) How is it that this matter of Moving the Heavens is considered so particularly to threaten the Unity of Allah, and that that Unity is only saved when He is relieved from even the function of Commanding the (outermost) Heaven to be moved?

(9) And who is this Commander who thus commands, and who orders all things, and who is related to pure Being as the Sun to Elemental Light? And what was "the mystery (in this affair), the disclosure of which this book does not admit of"?

(10) What becomes of a Deity of whom nothing whatsoever can even be said or predicated? And how, then, can a "relation" between Him and His Vicegerent be asserted, still more described as above? And how can this Unknowable, Unimaginable and Inconceivable be nevertheless "reached" by mystic souls?

---

[1] This is all the more marked because the words are Ghazzâlî's own gloss on a quotation from the Koran; see below.
[2] E.g. Tahâfut, pp. 57, 60

(11) What was "the book" into which Ghazzâlî himself says he put all his esoteric teaching (Jawâhir, p. 31); which he implores any into whose hands it may fall not to publish; which Ibn Ṭufail denies could have been this Mishkât (Ḥayy, ed. Gautier, pp. 13-15, trans. Gautier. pp. 12-14), nor any other of the supposed esoteric books that "had come to Andalus"?

THE PROBLEM OF THE VICEGERENT IN IBN RUSHD AND IBN TUFAIL

AFTER this it will cause no surprise that it is this figure of the Vicegerent (al-Muṭâ` . . . alladhî amara bi taḥrîk il-samâwât) who excited the curiosity and suspicion of thinkers in the century after Ghazzâlî's death. The passage is at least twice singled out, once by Ibn Rushd in the treatise already cited, and once by Ibn Ṭufail in his Ḥayy ibn Yaqẓân.

(1) Ibn Rushd uses the passage to level at Ghazzâlî a direct accusation of gravest hypocritical insincerity over a matter which Ghazzâlî had ostentatiously singled out as the prime test of orthodoxy, namely, the doctrine of emanation. According to Ibn Rushd the passage about the Vicegerent was the explicit teaching of this doctrine of the Philosophers, for which, elsewhere, Ghazzâlî can find no words strong enough to express his censure and contempt. The words of Ibn Rushd are as follows:

"Then he comes on with his book known as Mishkât al-Anwâr, and mentions therein all the grades of the Knowers of Allah; and says that all of them are veiled save those who believe that Allah is not the mover of the First Heaven, He being the One from Whom this mover of the First Heaven emanated: which is an open declaration on his part of the tenet of the philosophers' schools in the science of theology; though he has said in several places that their science of theology (as distinct from their other sciences) is a set of conjectures.[1]

It is not within the scope of this Introduction to follow in detail the evidence for and against the truth of this radical accusation. This has been done at length and with considerable minuteness in the monograph in Der Islâm, which has already been cited (pp. 133-145). The reader must be referred to that; and it must suffice here to say that after the full consideration of all the evidence the verdict given there is Not Guilty. On the other hand, the existence of an esoteric doctrine in regard to this Vicegerent and his function is undeniable (and undenied); and it is clear, from the comparison of the Mishkât itself with the Munqidh, that that doctrine differed vitally from the one professed by Ghazzâlî exoterically (Munqidh, p. 11). Ghazzâlî himself, in a passage of remarkable candour,[2] admits that every "Perfect" man has three sets of opinions (madhâhib), (a) those of his own environment, (b) those he teaches to inquirers according as they are able to receive them, and (c) those which he believes in secret between himself and Allah, and never mentions except to an inner circle of friends or students.

Ibn Rushd's accusation was an attempt to identify the figure of the Vicegerent, al-Muṭâ` with that of Al Ma`lûl al Awwal, the First Caused, in the emanational scheme of the Neoplatonizing [3] philosophers of Islâm, with al-Fârâbî and Ibn Sinâ at their head.

---

[1] Op. cit., ed. Müller, p. 21, Cairo edition, p. 59. The treatise was written before A.H. 575; date of Mishkât c. 500.]
[2] Mîzân al `Amal, p. 214.
[3] The unquestionable Neoplatonism of much of the forms and expression of Ghazzâlî's thought, if not of the thought itself {p. 20} (see especially pp. 15, 16. 29, 47 seq.]), exposed him in a very special

This was the Demiurge, the Being who first emanates from the Absolute Being, and mediates between It and all the lower stages or relational existence, with their increasing limitedness and grossness, thus relieving the predicateless Absolute from all part in the creation or administration of the universe.

There can be no doubt that whatever Ghazzâlî's doctrine of the Vicegerent was, and whatever else his esoteric doctrine contained, the emanational theory formed no part of that doctrine. For this particular piece of pseudo-metaphysics he appears to have had a very particular dislike and contempt; and if Ibn Rushd was really serious in levelling his accusation he can hardly be acquitted of being blinded by his bitter prejudice against "Abû Hâmid". The only possible ground for Ibn Rushd's accusation which I have been able to discover is as follows:--it is a fact that the extreme (ghulât) Imâmites did identify al-Rûh "The Spirit of Allah" with the First Emanation[1] If, as is contended hereafter, Ghazzâlî identified al-Mutâ` with Al-Rûh, and Ibn Rushd was aware of this, he may have thought, or been pleased to think, that Ghazzâlî therefore thought that al-Mutâ` was the First Emanation. This would be an indirect confirmation of the identification which it is attempted presently to prove, namely, al-Mutâ` = al-Rûh.

(2) We now pass to the other criticism of the passage, by Ibn Rushd's contemporary Ibn Tufail, in the introduction to his philosophical romance entitled Hayy Ibn Yaqzân.[2]

---

way to this charge of emanational pantheism. And it cannot have made it easier for him to steer clear of such dangers in fact.]

[1] Massignon, Hallâj, p. 661
[2] Ed. Gautier, pp. 14-15, transl. 12-14.

Ibn Tufâil's allusion to this perplexing passage is as follows:--

"Some later writers [1] have fancied they have found something tremendous in that passage of his that occurs at the end of al-Mishkât, which (they think) impales Ghazzâlî on a dilemma from which there is no escape. I mean where, after speaking of the various degrees of the

Light-Veiled, and then going on to speak of the true Attainers, he tells us that these Attainers have discovered that this Existing One possesses an attribute which negates unmitigated Unity; insisting that it necessarily follows from this that Ghazzâlî believed that the Absolute Being has within His Essence some sort of plurality: which God forbid!"

The excursus on this passage in the article cited from Der Islâm (pp. 145-151) can only be summarized here. It seems to have escaped the critics quoted by Ibn Tufail, that the Unveiled, according to Ghazzâlî himself, abandoned the position of the last of the Light-Veiled just because of this dread, viz. that the identification of al-Mutâ` with Allah would endanger "the unmitigated Unity" of Deity. Ibn Tufail himself, though he admits the serious contradictions which appear in Ghazzâlî's books, flatly refuses to see in this passage anything so monstrous, or anything sinister at all.

Unfortunately he does not give us his own exegesis of the passage; but it may perhaps be inferred from his own schematization of the grades of being. In this he makes elaborate use of the schema of reflectors, and reflectors of reflectors, which Ghazzâlî has already suggested in this book (pp. [15, 16]). "The

---

[1] Or "a later writer" presumably Ibn Rushd himself, in the passage already cited and discussed.

essences of the Intelligences of the Spheres" are represented as successive, graded reflections of the Divine Essence. The highest of them is not the essence of the One Real nor is he the Sphere itself, nor is he other than both. He is, as it were, the image of the sun which appears in a polished mirror; for that image is neither the sun, nor the mirror, nor other than them both." It is probable that Ibn Ṭufail, who professed to have won through to his position after studying al-Ghazzâlî and Ibn Ṣînâ (the juxtaposition is singular!), would have more or less equated this conception of the highest Essence of the Intelligences of the Spheres with the conception of al-Muṭâ` in the Mishkât, though he says nothing about the business of Heaven-moving in relation to this Being. It need not follow that al-Ghazzâlî would have accepted this explanation[1]; though both men were evidently striving equally to avoid a total pantheism, and both disbelieved in the emanational theory as taught by al-Fârâbî and Ibn Sinâ.

---

[1] Though his "mirror" schema in Mishkât, p. [15], is near Ibn Ṭufâil's meaning.

ONE SOLUTION OF THE PROBLEM OF THE VICEGERENT

IN the absence of "the book" into which Ghazzâlî put these secret opinions, or inconceivable mysteries, including, we may suppose, the secret of this mysterious Vicegerent, we are not likely to reach any authoritative settlement of the question: nor, even if we be put on the right track, clear up the whole of the mystery. For want of direct help from our author, therefore, the only thing to be done is to examine minutely al-Mishkât itself, to see if it yields any indirect help. It would seem that from this examination two possible solutions emerge. In this section the first of these will be discussed.

This solution, which was first suggested to the writer by the distinguished French Orientalist, M. Louis Massignon, identifies the mysterious figure of this Vicegerent, al-Mutâ`, with the Qutb ("Axis") or some other Supreme Adept. According to the developed doctrine, this Qutb was an earthly Mystic of supremest attainment, who during his lifetime administered the affairs of the heavens and the earth. There was nothing about him, during his lifetime, to suggest to any observer that he was, engaged in so stupendous a task, and it was not known till after his death that he had been "the Axis of his time" (qutbu zamânihi).

The beginnings of this doctrine go back far beyond al-Ghazzâlî-- a rudimentary form of it was held by even the ultra-orthodox Hanbalites,[1] and a developed form of the conception is

---

[1] Massignon, Passion d' al-Hallâj, p. 754.

expressed quite definitely in al-Hujwîrî's Kashf al-Mahjûb,[1] and must have been widely held, in orthodox circles too, in the fifth century, at the close of which our treatise was written.

Moreover, at least from the time of al-Hallâj, to whom, as we shall see, our author in this treatise refers in terms by no means of repudiation, the very word under discussion, al-Mutâ` or some other form of the same verb, occurs in significant connexion with supreme sainthood. One of the accusations levelled against al-Hallâj was that he taught that "having attained to sainthood the Adept becomes al-Mutâ` he who says to a thing 'Be!' and it becomes".[2] It sounds startling enough, but it was a true accusation, though it has to be taken in connexion with the whole of Hallâj's philosophy of mystical union with the Divine.[3] For he did definitely adopt from a predecessor, Ibn `Iyâd, the aphorism "Man atâ`a Allaha atâ`ahu kullu shay'",[4] an aphorism which received a later redaction (quite in the spirit of Hallâj, as has been shown), "man hudhdhi-ba ... fa yasîru mutâ`an, yaqûlu lish shay'i `Kun' fa yakûn," "He who has passed through the mystic askesis becomes Obeyed; he says to this or that, 'Be!' and it is."[5]

Since then al-Hallâj did so teach, and did use this very word, and since al-Ghazzâlî in this treatise betrays a very considerable admiration of al-Hallâj, and a sort of tremulous half-assent to

---

[1] p. 214 of trans.
[2] Massignon, op. cit., p. 791; ib., p. 472.
[3] The sense in which he did use the expression, and the proof that it did not in his thought mean self-deification, is given very clearly in Massignon, op. cit., 519-521.
[4] Op. cit., p. 472.
[5] Al-Avnî on al-Istakhrî., quoted in a letter by M. Massignon to the writer.

his wildest utterances, including the notorious "Ana-l Haqq" itself, it would seem that a strong prima-facie case has been made out for identifying the Mutâ` of our treatise, in spite of the cosmic nature of his functions, with some supreme Adept. But only a prima-facie case. To make out the thesis itself, the treatise itself must be interrogated; for it by no means follows that because a Hallâj held an opinion a Ghazzâlî adopted it.

There are, certainly, some passages that do suggest that the solution is along this line.

(1) The description of the adventures of a soul in highest state of Union (Mish., p. [24]) tends to bear out the Identification, or the general idea underlying it. The person there described is a supreme Adept, and in particular al-Hallâj himself. Having reached Union with the One divine Real, he ascends in and with Him "to the throne of the Divine Unity and from thenceforth administers the Command throughout His (or 'his,' for in this extraordinary passage the pronouns remain the same throughout) storied Heavens." The words translated "administers the Command", yudabbîru-l amr, are remarkable, for they contain an Arabic word (amr) which, as we shall see presently, is to the last degree significant, being the very word used in the Mutâ` passage (p. [55]), where Ghazzâlî confesses it is an obscure mystery. The Mutâ` (Commander) is said to move the outermost Heaven by precisely the amr (command). The words yudabbîru-l amr could no doubt be translated in a less significant way, owing to the troublesome double meaning of amr, ("affair," "command"), namely, "he disposes things." But in view of the fact that this amr was a notable Sûfî term, and a mysterious problem alluded to by Ghazzâlî in this very treatise, it seems inevitable to take it as "command" here. And a "Command" necessitates an "Obeyed".

(2) On p. [23], where the reference throughout is purely general, and presumably applies to anyone who has the necessary qualifications and attains this supreme mystical "state", Ghazzâlî says that when the mystic Ascent is complete, "if there be indeed any change, it is by way of 'the Descent into the Lowest Heaven', the radiation from above downwards." This also suggests supreme divine activity in the Universe below, especially if the word ishrâq refers, as it probably does, to causative activity.

(3) On pp. [13, 14] occurs another passage which strongly supports the general identification, though it leaves its particular and personal reference still obscure. In this the adepts, who in their mystical Ascent (mi`râj) "attained to that supreme attainment", are said to be "the Prophets", who "from thence looked down upon the entire World Invisible [precisely the world of the Heavens]; for he who is in the world of the Realm Supernal is which Allah, and hath the keys of the Unseen. I mean that from where he is descend the causes of existing things; for the world of sense is one of the effects of yonder-world of causes", etc. This looks almost like a reasoned, philosophic doctrine behind the mystical one, that to attain to the world of Reality is ipso facto to attain to the fount of causation; which involves the ability to direct the Causes which control all the Effects in the Heavens below and the Earth beneath. The Vicegerent does no more than this.

A close scrutiny of these passages leaves, one, nevertheless, with the impression that the Adepts whose celestial adventures are there described are too generalized, or perhaps one should say too pluralized, to be identifiable with this single, solitary figure of al-Mutâ` as he is presented in our passage. As far as these three passages go, this assumption of the reins of the Universe is only granted to Adepts in their mystic "States", to Prophets in their highly exceptional "Ascent". There is nothing to show that two or more such Attainers might not exist at one time, or that even one must always be existing; in other words, there is no trace of the complete and fully developed Quṭb doctrine in this treatise. But these considerations make it impossible to identify any one of these Adepts, or all of them together, with the cosmic al-Muṭâ`, whose function, related as it is to the very mechanism of the Heavens, is ceaseless, and coextensive with Time itself. And these last four words suggest a further consideration which in itself seems fatal to the proposed identification; namely, that al-Muṭâ` was Vicegerent from the very foundation of the world; he is the one "who commanded the Heavens to be moved" (p. [55, l. 12]). No Ḥallâj, no Adept, no Quṭb, no Prophet even, ever claimed, or had claimed for him, such priority as this,[1] or even priority at all. But if not, none of them--and, if so, no terrestrial being at all--can claim to fill the role of this Vicegerent. The three passages were probably intended only to assert and account for the karâmât of the Saints in their wonder-working which was parallel to that of the Koranic Jesus.

The a-priori question of our author's attitude to the Quṭb doctrine--whether, consistently with his published writings, he could have sustained such a doctrine in this work--is one which can only be indicated here. Professors R. Nicholson and D.S. Macdonald have both communicated to the writer, in reference to the passage under discussion, their opinion that there is an a-priori impossibility. To al-Ghazzâlî the doctrine was tainted with

---

[1] The question of the priority claimed by a certain school for Mohammed, and of the nûr Muḥammadi, will be considered, later.

Imâmism, his special bete noire (see his attack on the Ta`lîmites in his Munqidh;[1] that since an omnipotent.

Administrator must also be an infallible Guide (whom Ghazzâlî would not have at any price), there is no room for the former in Ghazzâlî's thought (thus Professor Macdonald). If the Muṯâ` is not Mohammed, he is certainly no Saint (thus Professor Nicholson).

Be this as it may, the above considerations, drawn from the study of the text itself, and from the passages which prima facie seemed to point to the Quṯb-Muṯâ` identification, seem finally, when more closely examined, to rule that identification out.

---

[1] See Nicholson, The Idea of Personality in Ṣûfism, p. 46

ANOTHER SOLUTION

BUT there are other passages in our treatise which, when carefully studied, lead to the belief that in Ghazzâlî's own mind--though the identification is nowhere explicitly stated or significantly hinted--the Mutâ` is none than al-Rûh, THE SPIRIT OF ALLAH.[1]

In S. 17, 87, Mohammed himself had left this enigmatic entity as a divinely uncommunicated, and therefore incommunicable, mystery. The passage runs as follows: "They ask thee of The Spirit: say, The Spirit pertains to my Lord's Word-of-Command, and ye have not been communicated knowledge [of It] save a little." The Arabic of the words italicized is min amri rabbî; and we are again faced, at the outset, with the troublesome double meaning of the word amr. The phrase min amr might merely mean--perhaps did only mean--"a matter of"[2] (my Lord's), a vague phrase, common in Arabic, meaning "something that pertains to" so and so. But in a case like this, we are not concerned with what Mohammed may originally have meant, but what mystic writers have taken him to mean. And enormously though this verse attracted puzzled, and baffled commentators and mystics of all ages, the latter seem to have taken the

---

[1] Nicholson. The Idea of Personality in Sûfism, pp. 44, 45. The identification had occurred independently to the present writer before appearance of Professor Nicholson's work. It had also occurred independently to Professor D. B. Macdonald.

[2] The word min is itself tantalizingly ambiguous. It might mean "(derived) from" or "(part) of" or "pertaining to." Under such circumstances one looks round for the vaguest possible phrase to render the preposition.

word amr, with practical unanimity, in the far more significant sense of "Command". The Hebrew root means "speak", and this meaning is implicit in the Arabic root also, which signifies spoken command. And just as later Jewish writers made out of a derivative of this root a Logos doctrine (Memra), so the Mohammedan mystics came near to making a Logos doctrine out of the word amr, taking their start from this very text.

A mystery having been definitely started by this text, a haze of mystification was thrown over the entire subject of "spirit": over angels as "spirits", over the human "spirit", the prophetic "spirit"; the interrelation between these, and the relation of all to "the Spirit"; finally Its relation to Allah. In our treatise there is a full measure of this mystification.

"The Spirit" is ar-Rûh. With this may be absolutely identified Rûh Allah "The Spirit of God"; Rûhuhu "His Spirit"; and al-Rûhu-l Qudsî[1] (or Rûhu-l Qudsî) "The Transcendent Spirit"--all Koranic expressions.

What then are the considerations which suggest that we have in this Figure of Mystery the key to the mystery of the Vicegerent? On this supposition there would be no wonder that Ghazzâlî left the figure of the latter a mystery, and declined to divulge the secret of it (p. [55]). He could not divulge the whole secret, because by the decree of Allah and the Book, he could not know it himself--"save a little." And, there is no wonder he declined to discuss it, considering the interminable complexities and baffling obscurities of the recorded musings of Sûfî doctors on the theme.

---

[1] This is the Arabic for the Christian "The Holy Spirit". But in Arabic as in early Hebrew the word emphasized the idea of separation or transcendence rather than of righteousness or holiness.

At the very outset we are struck by the fact that the word Muṭâ` occurs in the Koran (S. 81, 23), and not only so, but it occurs as an attribute of the mysterious Agent of Revelation, the vision of whom Mohammed saw at the first (S. 53, 5-16). The text 87, 23, is not definitely cited in Mishkât; and in later Islâm the commentators, with their arid tameness, made a stereotyped identification of this Figure with the Angel Gabriel. But the Koran gives no warrant for this; and there is nothing in the Mishkât to show that Ghazzâlî thus taught. On the contrary, Gabriel is assigned a low place in the angelic hierarchy. No one can read those two Koranic passages (in S. 87 and S. 53) without feeling that Mohammed's awful visitant on those two occasions was the One of absolute supreme rank in the heavenlies: not a spirit but the Spirit. And It was muṭâ`--"one who is obeyed." Is it not but a very short step from this to al-Muṭâ`, The Obeyed-One?

The identification, however attractive, would nevertheless be precarious if there was not so much in the Mishkât itself that supports this identification.

(1) On p. [15] the ultimate kindling-place of the graded Lights, of which the Prophets occupy the lower and terrestrial ranks and the Angelic Beings the higher and celestial, is the theme of discussion. Both these ranks of beings are compared to "lights" and all of them are contrasted with the Highest of all, who is compared to "fire", from whose flame these graded lights are successively lit, from top to bottom. Who and what is this Highest of all next to Allah? He is said to be an Angel with countenances seventy thousand'. . . {p. 37} This is he who is contrasted with all the angelic host, in the words: 'On that day whereon THE SPIRIT ariseth, and the Angels, rank on rank.'" It is thus explicitly clear that this Being is the highest of all possible beings in heaven or earth next to Allah; and so, if the Vicegerent

of p. [55] is also the highest of all, it would seem inevitable to equate them.

(2) In the very next page, p. [16], Ghazzâlî schematizes this conception, and, comparing Allah with the Sun (the source of light in the terrestrial system), he compares the highest of the ministrant lights to the Moon (all others being reflections, or reflections-of-reflections, of it). This "Highest is the one who is nearest to the Ultimate Light: . . . that Nighest to Allah, he whose rank comes nighest to the Presence Dominical, which is the Fountainhead of all these Lights" This "Nighest" and "Highest" cannot be other than THE SPIRIT spoken of in the preceding page. And on p. [31]--unless Ghazzâlî has suddenly changed all the symbols--the Sun is said to be the Sovereign, while "the antitype of the Moon will be that Sovereign's Minister (wakîl), for it is through the moon that the sun sheds his light on the world in its own absence, and even so it is through his own wakîl that the Sovereign makes his influence felt by subject who never beheld the royal person". Does not this wakîl who stands "highest and nighest" to his Liege-Lord, and who makes himself obeyed by all that Lord's subjects, strongly suggest "the Obeyed One", al-Mutâ`, the Vicegerent of the conclusion, whose function is, precisely, this?

(3) But what perhaps clinches the matter is the tell-tale word amr in that passage about al-Mutâ` himself on p. [55]. Those who stopped short of complete illumination, he says, identified al-Mutâ` with Allah just because he moves the primum mobile (and so all things) "with his Word of Command" (amr). "The explication of which amr (he continues), and what it really is, contains much that is obscure, and too difficult for most minds, besides going beyond the scope of this book." And then he says that the perfect Illuminati perceived that, al-Mutâ` the Obeyed One is not more than the Highest--other-than-Absolute-Deity, and is related to Him as the sun to Essential Light (mysterious

enough this!) or as a glowing coal to the Elemental Fire: and therefore they turned their faces from that Being "who commanded (amara) the moving of the Heavens" to the One Existent, Transcendent, Incomparable, Predicateless.

With this word amr thus impressed on us with such penetrating significance we turn back to the Koran text: "The Spirit pertains to my Lord's Word of Command (amr) . . ." Unless the word min introduces a quite upsetting element, the identification between this SPIRIT and the Commander who is Obeyed seems complete.

But the history of the Sûfî teaching on the text shows that min need introduce no such upsetting element, and that the practical identification of Amr with Rûḥ, of The Word of Command with The Spirit, was with the Mystics a familiar idea. It was the explicit teaching of al-Hallâj[1] and the typical "word of command" which this Divine Spirit gave was the fiat "Kun!" "Be!"[2] We have seen the fascination which this treatise shows al-Hallâj had for al-Ghazzâlî. Does it not seem likely, nay almost certain, that in his meditation on the inscrutable text he followed al-Hallâj in this equation, with whatever mental reserve regarding the Spirit itself--whether divine or creaturely, eternal or originate? Not that it was only Imâmites or extreme Sûfî Sunnites like al-Hallâj who asserted the divinity of The Spirit. The ultra-orthodox Hanbalites "admitted in some manner

---

[1] Massignon, op. cit., pp. 519-21.
[2] This mediation of the creative function would carry with it the mediation of the administrative. In this connexion use would unquestionably be made of S. 7, 53, "the sun, the moon, and the stars are compelled-to-work by His amr--His Word-of-Command--His Spirit--exactly the function of al-Muṭâ`.

the eternity of the Rûḥ Allah".[1] Ibn Ḥanbal himself had given them the lead with a characteristic hedging aphorism (which reminds us of similar remarks on the Ṣifat, the Kalâm Allah, and the Qur'ân) "Whoever says that al-Rûḥ is created, (makhlûq) is a heretic: whoever says that It is eternal (qadîm) is an infidel."[2] His followers held fast on to "uncreate", and it was hard to keep "eternal" from following. No wonder al-Ghazzâlî gave a unique and mysterious tinge to his similitude for "The Obeyed", and that It figures, virtually, as an Arian Logos. The more one reflects on what is said about the function of this Being in M., p. [55], and especially Its comparison with the Sun (Allah being Essential Light), or with glowing coal (Allah being Elemental Fire), the more unique It appears, and the more mysterious our author's thought about It becomes. For such functions, and such a relation to Absolute Deity, are in very truth entirely unique, in kind as well as degree; and, thus described, the Vicegerent becomes, in a secondary way, as unique a Figure as is Deity Itself. No wonder the passage raised doubts as to the soundness of our author's monotheism! No wonder he was not anxious to go more deeply into the matter, out of consideration for the limited spiritual capacities of his readers! Perhaps, to preserve his own faith in the Unity, Indivisibility, and absolute Uniqueness of Allah, he was glad to leave the dark problem of the Vicegerent where Allah Himself had left that of--the Spirit--an uncommunicated and incommunicable mystery, which now he only knew in part, and only saw as in a glass, darkly.

It remains to consider whether there is any evidence that Ghazzâlî extended the equation Mutâ` = Amr = Rûḥ to include the Nûr Muhammadî (as suggested tentatively by Professor R. Nicholson in his lectures on "The Idea of Personality in Ṣûfism"[3]),

---

[1] Massignon, op. cit., p. 664.
[2] Ib., p. 661.
[3] Pp. 46, 47, and Lecture III.

the archetypal spirit of Mohammed, the Heavenly Man created in the image of God, and regarded as a Cosmic Power on whom depends the order and preservation of 'the universe. If this could be sustained it would to some extent modify the conclusion reached before that al-Mutā` had nothing to do with any human being, idealized or not, whether a Prophet or even Mohammed; though even so, there would be a vast difference between this archetypal Spirit and the historical Prophet.

While the germs of this idea, as of every other one, may be found much earlier than Ghazzâlî's century (the fifth), the study of the sketch which M. Massignon gives of the history of the doctrine (Hallâj, pp. 830 seqq.) does not create the impression that it was developed or received in orthodox circles[1] up to Ghazzâlî's time. Professor Nicholson does not find it in an orthodox Sûfî writer earlier than `Abdu-l Qâdir al-Jîlânî (b. 571, d. 561), in the generation immediately succeeding that of Ghazzâlî.[2] After which the doctrine developed and spread amazingly, reaching its height with Ibn al-`Arabî al-Jîlî several centuries later.[3]

Thus the a-priori evidence is this time decidedly against Ghazzâlî's having anything to do with this doctrine. Unless, therefore, very clear actual evidence were found in his writings, it would be surely justifiable to assert definitely that it is not Ghazzâlîan. It appears not to be found in his works other than al-Mishkât. If this is so, it may be further asserted with confidence that it is not found in al-Mishkât either. On the

---

[1] It was at first prevalently Imâmite and Shî`ite (Nicholson, Idea of Personality in Sûfism, p. 58).
[2] He described Muhammed as al-rûh al-qudus and rûh jasad al-wajûd "the Transcendent Spirit, the Spirit of the body of the Universe."
[3] Nicholson, op. cit., p. 59.

contrary, there is much there that shows a relatively simple, primeval conception of Mohammed on the part of Ghazzâlî. For him the archetypal man is Adam, as in the Koran, not Mohammed.[1] An examination of the passage[2] in which the idea of the "Khalîfa" appears shows that here also his thought was not esoteric, and that Mohammed was not in his mind: he is thinking of the whole human race, or of Adam himself, the first and representative human being, the only "Khalîfa" particularized by the Koran. And the one passage in the Mishkât which at first sight does look as if it contained a "high doctrine of the person" of Mohammed, turns out on closer inspection to, prove the exact reverse, viz. that essential-ly be belonged to this world and to the time-order--to the prophets, above whom are ranked the celestial "Lights" culminating, as we have seen, in the Supreme Angelical, The Spirit. This passage is on pp. [14, 15]. Here we have the Transcendent Spirit Prophetical (al-Rûḥ al-qudus al-nabawî) attributed to Mohammed as prophet, by reason of which he is called a Luminous Lamp (sirâj munîr). If this stood by itself we might be suspicious of something esoteric. But immediately after this the other prophets, and even saints, are said to be "Lamps"', and to possess, as Its name implies this Spirit Prophetical. The sequel shows that this Spirit is the Fire from which all the Angelical lights above and the Prophetical lights beneath are lit, and that this Spirit is the Supreme Angelical, "The Spirit," as in the passage already discussed.[3]

---

[1] M., p. [34].

[2] M., p. [22].

[3] See above, pp. 36-37 The only thing that puzzles is that Ghazzâlî sometimes distributes and pluralizes the Spirit, see p. [15, l. 4] and p. [22. l. 8]. In each case the regulative singular, however, is close by. This reminds one of Rev. iv, 5 and v. 6, compared with Rev. ii. 7.

To sum up the conclusion to which I have been led by a consideration of the evidence of the Mishkât itself, top-ether with the a-priori evidence which supplements it and is checked by it,--the heavenly Vicegerent is the Spirit of Allah, the Transcendent Spirit of Prophecy, the divine Word-of-Command; he is not a Quṯb or any Adept; he is not Mohammed nor the archetypal spirit of Mohammed.

Whether this mystery of the Vicegerent was connected in our author's mind with that of the divine-human, archetypal Ṣûra, as developed by al Hallâj and other advanced Mystics, will be discussed later.

AL-GHAZZALI AND THE SEVEN SPHERES

THE Seven Planetary Heavens played a great part in Platonic,[1] Neoplatonic, and Gnostic-theosophical schemes. The naive adoption by Mohammed (in the Koran) of the Ptolemaic celestial construction was one of the things which added picturesqueness to early Mohammedan tradition and theology; caused endless trouble to generations of later theologians; made it easier for Neoplatonic ideas to graft themselves on to Islam; gave to the raptures of the Mystics sensuous form and greater definition; and afforded to the Philosophers a line of defence, and even of attack, in their war with the Theologians [2] And the allusions of the Koran were heavily reinforced by the legend of the Mirâj, the exact origin of which is obscure, but which appears in a highly developed form almost from the first. The influences of the Mi`râj are indeed evident in page after page of the Mishkât.

Al-Ghazzâlî's sympathies in regard to this subject were divided. He disliked the Philosophers, and this made him displeased with their confident assertions about the Heavens, while he detested the "philosophical" profit to which they put them. On the other hand, he was a Ṣûfî and thus in closest touch with persons who made very similar assertions about the Heavens, and also put them to profit in their own way. Finally, he was an Ash`arite Theologian, belonging to a school which had recently, after much trouble, eliminated from theology the dangerous ideas to

---

[1] See the Vision of Er in the Republic, bk. X
[2] See Averroes' Ki tab al Kashf an manâhij al adillâ, quoted above on p. 11, note 2

which Mohammed's naive attitude to the Heavens, had given rise.

This uncertainty of touch comes out, as, might be expected, in a treatise like al-Mishkât with its blend of scholasticism and Neoplatonically-tinctured mysticism. The Heavens figure continually in its pages. They seem to play a most important part both in thought and in experience--towards the close of the book a determining part. Yet it is impossible to make out exactly what that part was, in the mind of al-Ghazzâlî himself.

On p. [23] we have a correlation of the human microcosm and the macrocosm of the celestial realm, Ptolemaically construed, in describing the Ascension of a God-united soul. The adept's body-and-soul structure is conceived of as subsisting in three planes or Spheres, which are correlated with the three lower spheres of the Seven Planetary Heavens. From the highest of these (the Intelligence) the soul takes its departure and ascends through the four upper Heavens (ila saba`i ṭabaqât) to the Throne [beyond the outermost Heaven]. Thus he "fills all things"' by his upward Ascent just as Allâh did by His downward Descent (nuzûl). In all this the pronoun "he" stands for the soul who is now Allâh-possessed and united, as described in what immediately precedes. It is the upward ascent of Allah (corresponding to His nuzûl illa-l samâ'i-l dunyâ), and not of the Adept only.

On the other hand, in p. [29], this Ascent is described in purely psychological terms, without this schema of the Heavens. And on p. [13] we have the following: "Do not imagine that I mean by the World Supernal the World of the [Seven] Heavens, though they are 'above' in respect of part of our world of sense-perception. {p. 49} These Heavens are equally present to our apprehension and that of the lower animals. But a man finds the doors of the Realm Celestial closed to him, neither does be become of or belonging to that Realm (mala-kûtî), unless this earth to him 'be changed into that which is not earth; and likewise the heavens;'[1] . . . and his 'heaven' come to be all that transcends his sense. This is the first Ascension for every Pilgrim who has set out on his Progress to the nearness of the Presence Dominical." And he continues: "The Angels ... are part of the World of the Realm Celestial, floating even in the Presence of the Transcendence, whence they gaze down upon our world inferior.

The last lines hardly give us the same ultra-spiritualizing impression which is conveyed by their predecessors. And, as we have already seen (Introduction, pp. 12-17), the part played by the Spheres with their Angels in the last section of the book is decisive, and there does not seem to be there any spiritualizing whatever.

How far, therefore, these passages are mere word-play, pious picturesqueness, or how far they represent speculation of a rather far-reaching character, is one of the puzzles of the book. In the Tahâfut, demolishing the arrogant claim of the Philosophers to prove their doctrine of the Spheres by syllogistic demonstration (burhân), he said: "The secrets of The Kingdom are not to be scanned by means of such fantastic imaginations as these; Allâh gives none but His Prophets and Saints (anbiyâ' and awliyâ') to scan them, and that by inspiration, not by demonstration. [2] So then there were mysteries and secrets in regard to the Spheres. In the Mishkât we are able to see pretty clearly that Ghazzâlî had his; but we are not able to see just what they were. He has kept this secret well.

---

[1] S. 14, 48
[2] Tah., p. 60. Quoted in the writer's article in Der Islâm, see pp. 134-6, 151, 152, where parts of the subject are gone into in greater detail.

41

ANTHROPOMORPHISM AND THEOMORPHISM IN AL-MISHKAT

THE doctrine of mukhâlafa--that the divine essence and characteristics wholly and entirely "differ from" the human-- appears to be assorted, as this treatise's last word, in its most extreme and intransigent form. For the conclusion of the whole matter, the end of the quest for truth for those who "Arrive", is "an Existent who transcends ALL that is comprehensible by human Insight . . . transcendent of and separate from every characterization that in the foregoing we have made."[1]

Nevertheless, the Mishkât itself seems to be one long attempt to modify or even negate this its own bankrupt conclusion. Indeed, it goes unusual lengths in asserting a certain ineffable likeness between Allâh and man. It is true that the usual anthrop-

---

[1] In Ghazzâlî the most extreme Agnosticism and the most extreme Gnosticism meet, and meet at this point; for, as he says (p [25]), things that go beyond one extreme pass over to the extreme opposite." For him "Creed because Incredible" becomes "Gnosis because Agnoston". What saved the Universe for him from his nihilistic theologizing was his ontology (see below, pp. 108 seqq.). What saved God for him from his obliterating agnosticism was the experience of the mystic leap, his own personal mi`râj. This may have been non-rational, but it was to him experience. Even those who regard the sensational experience of Sûfism as having been pure self-hypnotism cannot condemn them and the sense of reality they brought, in relation to the man who had thought his way out of both atheism and pantheism, and yet would have been left at the end of the quest, by his thinking alone, with an Unknown and Unknowable Absolute.]

omorphic expressions--the Hand, the Sessions on the Throne, the Descent to the Lowest Sphere, etc., those perennial sources for Moham-medan theologizing-are used and are discounted in the usual way. But they are, in reality, only discounted by being replaced by a S̲ûfî system of theomorphism. This has three main aspects--

(1) a quasi-Platonic doctrine of terrestrial type and celestial antitype;

(2) the relation of the divine and human rûh̲ (spirit);

(3) the relation of the divine and human s̲ûra ("image," "form").

(1) The whole of the first two parts of the treatise are practically an exposition of an Islamico-Platonic typology. It is not explicitly said that earthly things are more or less faint copies of "the patterns of things in the heavens," though this is probably implicit in what is said, namely, that the heavenly realities (haqâ'iq), (ma`ânî), all have their symbols on earth. These symbols or types, as their Arabic term itself suggests (amthâl), do possess a "resemblance" to their celestial antitypes, for, as al Ghazzâlî remarks, "the thing compared (al-mushabbah, the antitype) is in some sort parallel, and bears resemblance, to the thing compared therewith (al-mushabbah bihi, the type or symbol), whether that resemblance be remote or near; a matter again which is unfathomably deep."[1] Ghazzâlî. can hardly be allowed to elude the application of this true principle to Allâh Himself, considering that this very Koran-verse which it is the object of the entire treatise to expound begins with a simile. "Light" is the chosen, or rather the God-given symbol, wherewith Allah is "compared", and which therefore He must "in

---

[1] M., p. 14.

some sort resemble". This analogy of light floods the whole book. Now Allah is the Sun: now the Light of lights: and at the end, in the same breath in which Abu Ḥâmid, with the incorrigible inconsistency which so angered Averroes, denied the validity of the similitude, description, relation, or even predication in regard to Allâh, we are told that He stands in relation to His Vicegerent (or "wakeel" in a parallel passage) as the pure Light-essence to the sun, or as the Elemental Fire to a glowing coal. Theomorphism has "in some sort" been admitted.

(2) In the Iḥyâ' al `Ulûm Ghazzâlî speaks of the human rûḥ as amr rabbâni "a divine affair" (amr must surely bear here its other meaning); and he is there very anxious, not to say agitated, over the esoteric character of the doctrine; it must be kept a dead secret from the Many! it must not be set forth in a book![1] "The specific characteristic which differentiates humanity [from the lower creation] is something which it is not lawful to indite in a book."[2] The thing that agitates him is the relation of this human rûḥ to the Spirit of God, rûḥ Allâh, and its relation to Allâh. The matter is esoteric--it is to be "grudged" to the "commons"--because it is dangerous ground. It is dangerous ground because one has to talk warily in order to avoid a violation of the uniqueness of Allâh, which would involve confusing Creator with created, and so passing gradually to ishrâk, which is the worst "infidelity."

This particular anxiety is not reflected in the present treatise; it is strange that the mystery of rûḥ does not figure in the list (see above, p. 5) over which the author's favete linquis! is inscribed. [3]

---

[1] See Mizân, p. 214, quoted above.
[2] Iḥyâ, iv, p. 294, quoted in a letter to the writer from Professor R. Nicholson.]
[3] The human 'aql does figure on that list, pp. [6, 7]

He is mainly occupied with working out what the New Testament calls the "operations", rather than the nature of the spirit. In so doing the singular "spirit" becomes plural "spirits", arwâḥ, which, as already observed, happens also in the Book of the Revelation. Ghazzâlî works out the theory of the several "spirits" of the human psychology; then the graded "spirits" of the heavenly hosts; and then the Neoplatonic or theosophic idea of the gradation of all these (in maqâmât), and the way in which they are "lit" (muqtabasa) from each other in order: we must not say "derived", for that would involve him in the emanationism be was ever anathematizing yet, for ever incurring the suspicion of.[1] In all this his tone is open, easy, confident. The special mystery of The Spirit had been already discounted in the Koran, so that was harmless. As for the identification of Rûḥ Muṭâ`, if our theory is correct, that was a grand secret. But that secret he never intended even to hint at, and it would really seem as if we had surprised and betrayed a sirr maknûn!

(3) It was the ṣûra tradition,[2] "ALLAH CREATED ADAM AFTER HIS IMAGE," that above all else led Moslem thinkers into temptation--the temptation of trenching on the uniqueness of Allâh. Its very riskiness seems, however, to have fascinated them supremely from the very outset. Not one of them could let it alone. In this very treatise Ghazzâlî returns to it again and again. Perhaps it would accord with inner truth to say rather that both he and others returned to that tradition not so much as moths fascinated by a dangerous glare, but as those who are feeling cold return for warmth and cheer to even an alien fire. The aphorism, sacred as a Koran text, was the assertion and pledge

---

[1] See the writer's op. cit. in Der Islâm, pp. 138-141.]

[2] Gen. i. 27, though Islâm ignores the parentage.

that man somehow is, or may become, "like God." The word ṣûra became the symbol and the guarantee of theomorphism.

In the first allusion in the Mishkât to this tradition (p. [9]), the point of the similarity is the human intelligence (`aql). In virtue of his intelligence, Ghazzâlî hints, man is "after the image of Allâh." The `aql is "Allâh's balance-scale upon earth."[1] In its own sphere it is infallible.[2] From the `aql, as from a firm "taking-off" place, souls make their mystic Ascension to the heavenlies.[3] It is because it is thus the specifically human faculty that it is a determinative element in the human ṣûra.[4]

The second allusion (M., p. [23]) carries us very much further-- even to that verge from which Moslem mystics so often looked dizzily down, but from which they so seldom fell, into the pantheistic abyss. Behold a human soul in completest Union (jam`) with Deity, sitting on The Throne, and administering all things in heaven and earth! "Well might one," says our author, "in looking upon such an one," get a new view of this tradition. Is not such a uniate, indeed, "after the image of Allâh"? But, he continues, "after contemplating that word more deeply one becomes aware that it has an interpretation like [al-Hallâj's] 'I am the One Real.[5] Unfortunately he has omitted to indicate

---

[1] M., p. [29]
[2] Ib., p. [10]
[3] Ib., p. [24]
[4] Ib., [40].
[5] How {to} translate this "Ana-l-Haqq"? Not by Jesus, "I am the Truth", tempting though this is. "I am the Absolute" would be a parallel rendering in modern philosophic parlance. Professor Nicholson's "I am God" is startling, but illuminating because perfectly justifiable: for al-Haqq and Allâh are mutually and exclusively convertible.]

what precisely that interpretation is. We have a tantalizing author to deal with.

What was that interpretation?

Probably we do not find it in the third passage (pp. [34, 35]), though it is deeply influenced by Hallâjian thought. There is in the celestial world something which "developpe, modalise, et concerte entre elles les creations divines ... une certaine structure interne particuliere a l'acte createur".[1] This living order, this organised "Presence" (hadar), is symbolized by the word Image, or Form. And this macrocosmic hadra has its earthly counterpart in an analogous human form, or sûra, which has the same "structure interne particuliere" (it is alluded to on p. [22, l. 1], and p. [34, l. 3], and described in detail on pp. [39-41]). Therefore, man, formed in this Form, is "after the Form, the Image, of this Merciful One (al Rahmân)". Ghazzâlî's explanation of his preference for this variation of the tradition, to which, however, he by no means always adheres, is difficult to follow. But the general idea clearly is that "but for this 'mercy' [i.e. of these two correlative and coincident Forms] every son of Adam would have been powerless to know his Lord, for 'only he who knows himself knows his Lord". The wheel has, indeed, brought us round a strange circle! Through the eternal grace of theomorphism we win back to a higher anthropomorphism, so that the proper study of God is--man!

---

[1] Massignon, op. cit., p, 519, describing Hallâj's doctrine of the divine rûh, and exactly hitting off Ghazzâlî's difficult thought on p. [24, ll. 2, 3], (cf. p, [22, l. 2]). But from this point of view rûh and sûra merge into each other, as a careful comparison of the two Mishkât passages just cited shows.

And this from the writer whose last word is that Allah must not have so much as an attribute predicated of Him, or the divine uniqueness will be violated! Truly, thus the whirligig of thought brings in his revenges.

We have already seen many indications that before he wrote this treatise Ghazzâlî must have been deep in the study of al-Hallâj; and the passage we have just been considering may be added to these indications. Yet there is no overt trace in it, or elsewhere in the Mishkât, of al-Hallâj's profoundest thought on this matter of the Divine-Adamic; no trace of that strange Figure--that Epiphany of humanized Deity, or Apotheosis of ideal-Humanity--which was presented by Allah to the angels for worship or ever the first man was created, and in which He Himself, on behalf of the human race, swore unto Himself the Covenant (mîthâq) of allegiance. For this conception, which has the closest interrelations with all the moments of the above discussion--rûh, amr, sûra, nûr-Muhammadî--the reader must be referred to the grand work which has brought to light so many hidden things, A Louis Massignon's La Passion d' Al Hosayn-ibn-Mansour al-Hallaj.[1] Ghazzâlî's silence on this so remarkable development of the Sûra tradition would suggest that it was precisely here that he felt it dangerous to follow al-Hallâj. What was possible for the seer might send the theologian over the line where Islam ends and pantheism begins. On the other hand, is it possible that here we have the explanation of our author's embarrassed words on p. [55] "on account of a

---

[1] Pages 485, 599-602. In a note Massignon hazards the tentative suggestion that this epiphanized God (called by al-Hallâj al-Nâsût) in contra-distinction from the unknowable al-Lâhût) is analogical to, or suggestive of Ghazzâlî's Vicegerent (p. 601, n. 5). The suggestion is thrilling, as we see. It must be repeated that there is no overt trace of the doctrine in M.]

Mystery which it is not in the competence of this book to reveal"? His inmost thought may have been, "Perhaps al-Hallâj has penetrated here to something of what the Koran itself [in the Spirit-Verse] left obscure. I neither assert, nor deny. Allâhu a`lam!"

Thus we come to the ultimate question--the ultimate question with every S̲ûfî writer and book--does he and it escape pantheism? What light comes from this "Niche for Lights" upon this obscure question?

PANTHEISM AND AL-GHAZZALI, IN AL-MISHKAT

THE root question in regard to al-Ghazzâlî, and every other advanced mystic and adept in Islâm, is the question of Pantheism: did he succeed in balancing himself upon the edge of the pantheistic abyss, and finding some foothold for his creationist theism, some position that cleared his conscience towards his orthodox co-religionists? Or did he fail in this? The Mishkât contains a good deal that is relevant to this final issue.

It contains much, in the first place, which on the face of it reads like naked pantheism; and in particular the whole passage on pp. [19, 20] and [22-4], where not only is the most extreme language of the extreme wing of Sûfism (Ana-l Haqq[1] and the rest) quoted with guarded approval, but there is open eulogy of the formula lâ huwa illâ Huwa "there is no it but HE", which is declared to be more expressive of real, absolute truth than the Mohammedan creed itself lâ ilâha ill-Allâh "there is no god but God". This would seem to be as unreserved an assertion of flat pantheism as could be found in philosophic Hinduism itself. Equally worthy of philosophic Hinduism is Ghazzâlî's "He is everything: He is that He is: none but He has ipseity or heity at all . . ."[9](p. [22]). And then gain the experience of the advanced Initiates and Adepts is described in terms of thorough pantheism: to them "the plurality of things fell away in its entirety. They were drowned in

---

[1] Which, it must be remembered, might not unfairly be translated -I am God---; see footnote above

the absolute Unitude[5] and their intelligences were lost in its abyss" (p. [19]); and when they return to earthly illusions again from that world of reality they "confess with one voice that they had seen nought existent there save the One Real (Allâh)". Existent! Do words mean what they say?

No, not precisely! with a Ghazzâlî, and with Mohammedan mystics, clinging desperately to orthodoxy! The matter, in fact, turns precisely on this word "existent". What is existence? What is non-existence? It was Ghazzâlî's ontological philosophy that seems to have yielded him a fulcrum on which he could precariously balance the pantheistic and the deistic moments of his religious thought.

This philosophy is poetically stated in our treatise, but in spite of the poetic, imaginative diction it can be recognized as identical with his usual doctrine.[1] It will be found on pp. [17-19, 21, 22]. We have there a picturesque representation of a doctrine well known to the schoolmen of Islâm, that Not-Being is a sort of dark limbo in which the Contingent awaits the creative word Kun "Be!"--compared in this "Light" treatise to a ray of light from the One Self-existing Being. Neither the Greeks nor the schoolmen could ever quite get over the feeling that, in predicating anything of Not-being or a Nonentity, in using the word "is" in a sentence with Not-being or a Nonentity as its subject, you have in some way ascribed, not existence, but a sort of quasi-being, to that subject. Hegel's solution was so to evacuate the category of mere, bare "Being" of all content, and to demonstrate its consequent total impoverishment and inanity, that it could be seen to be, the equivalent of Not-being.

---

[1] See, for example, Minqiah and the Lesser Madnûn (if that is Ghazzâlî's).]

This was impossible for the schoolmen, above all for Oriental schoolmen, even of the most contradictory schools, who regarded the category of "pure" being (they would never have said "mere") as the sublimest and most radiant of all the categories, and the very object of the whole quest of life. But the obverse of the Hegelian paradox may nevertheless be seen in their ascription to contingent not-yet-being a sort of quasi-existence. The effect of the creative word was simply to turn this potential into actual being. Thus the universe, always contingent, indeed but formerly potential-contingent, now became actual-contingent.

All this is schematized in al-Mishkât. The limbo becomes Darkness (p. 30); the potential-contingent, Dark Things; [1] the

---

[1] It is just here that, as it seems to the writer, the Philosophers with their Aristotelian doctrine of the eternity, the formless substrate of things--might well have forced a place for their thought, in spite of the Ghazzâlian wrath against them and it. For when the dark "self-aspect" of these contingencies of the Theologians is considered, prior to their "existence" (p. [59]), is there much to choose between the eternal potentiality asserted of them by Ghazzâlî, and the eternity asserted for hyle by the Philosophers? Ghazzâlî himself quotes a saying of Mohammed (p. [13]), on to which these Philosophers would eagerly have seized proving the point: "Allâh created the creation in darkness, then sent an effusion of His light upon it." For a man who was using this divine light-emanation to typify the act of creation, of calling out of non-being to being, it was dangerous surely to give, apparently so powerful an indication as this of a previous creation in "darkness" (= not being in Ghazzâlî's chosen symbology). It might very well have been claimed by the Philosophers that this creation-in-darkness is precisely their formless, chaotic hyle, eternal as darkness is eternal before the light shines. The Philosophers did pretend to prove their thesis from the Koran; see Averroes' Manâhij, ed. Müller, p. 13 (=Cairo ed. Faisafat Ibn Rushd, p. 12), where the following texts are cited in support, S. 11, 9; 14, 49; 41, 10.

divine creator, the Sun; the creative act, a Ray from His real being, whereby a dark Nonentity flashes into being and becomes an Entity, but an Entity that depends continuously on the permanent illumination of that ray, for in the Mohammedan creational scheme, at any rate, Creator is equally capable of being Annihilator.

At this point Ghazzâlî's tortured thought is greatly helped out by the ambiguous word wajh, which has two senses, or rather three, Face, Side, Aspect (logical). This gave him a formula: it was not the first time, nor the last, that the ambiguity of the chief word in a theological formula has been welcome to all concerned. He could take the Koran texts "the Wajh of everything faces (muwajjah) to Him and is turned in His direction," and "Whithersoever they turn themselves, there is the Wajh of Allâh;" and the ḥadîth qudsî, "Everything is a perishing thing except His Wajh;" and could then play on the word. In ancient and mediaeval times the merest plays on words were not considered figures of speech but profundities of thought. Quibbles masqueraded as discoveries. And so this word (a) enabled Ghazzâlî to keep his hold on creationism on the one hand, for these were "things" sure enough, all turned towards the central Sun and dependent for their existence on its creative light; and there was also the sound logical position, that under this aspect (wajh) of relatedness these things have actual being (p. [18]). So the actuality of the universe is saved, and the abyss of pantheism is avoided. And (b), on the other hand, he could say to the pantheistic Ṣûfî (and to himself in that mood), that equally under this "aspect" of relatedness things, if and when considered an sich, had no existence, were not existent at all. The only Existent was the Wajh Allâh (p. [22]) that is, Allâh Himself, for, as he carefully informs us (p. [19]), Allah cannot possibly be said to be greater" (akbar) than His own wajh; and must, therefore, be identical therewith. And thus the out-and-out pantheist might well feel his case complete; the last vestige of dualism disappears; Allah is All, and All is Allah, lâ mawjûda ill-Allâh (M. p. [18])! As Ghazzâlî himself put it, Allah is the Sun and besides the sun there is only the sun's light. Quid plura?

Nevertheless, it may be believed that Ghazzâlî himself contrived to use this ontology so as to keep, not lose, his hold on the reality[1] and actuality of things, and that early training, central theological orthodoxy, and strong commonsense proved by its help too strong for the pull towards pantheism, with which his late Sûfism with its Neoplatonic atmosphere and sensational ecstasies undoubtedly did pull him--as Sûfism pulled every Mohammedan mystical devotee. Is it not notable that even in the lyrical passages in this treatise, in which he describes (with a rather scared unction) the Mystics' intoxication and the verbal blasphemies which that state so happily permitted, and which were permitted to that state, Ghazzâlî keeps his head, and preserves the same cautious balance as he does in the ontological sections (see pp. [19, 20])? When these inebriates, he says, became sober again, "and they came under the sway of the intelligence . . . they knew that that had not been actual Identity, but only something resembling Identity" (not homoousion but homoiousion!). If we correctly translate ittihâd [2] thus, the remark is of crucial importance; for the ultimate test of a complete Pantheism is whether things are identical with God, or

---

[1] I.e. in the modern or western sense of the word, = "objectivity" To the mediaeval eastern thinker the Arabic word meant rather "ideality." It is a case of the difference between phenomenal and transcendental reality.]

[2] Professor Macdonald prefers "identification," to bring out the verb-aspect of the masdar more clearly.]

only united with Him. All classes of mystics without exception assert at least the latter--it is the "Union" of the Christian, as of the Muslim, Catholic; but only those who have actually surrendered their balance and toppled over into the pantheistic abyss assert the former. And Ghazzâlî did not do so. He goes on to quote yet another "drunken" cry of a soul in Union, "I am He whom I love, and He whom I love is I," and shows how even here a distinction is preserved. And then that other, who likened the Union to a transparent Glass filled with red Wine--

"The glass is thin, the wine is clear.
The twain are alike, the matter is perplexed
For 'tis as though there were wine and no wineglass there,
Or as though there were wine-glass and nought of wine."

And thus comments: "Here there is a difference between saying 'The wine is the wineglass' and "tis as though it were the wineglass'." The former, he tells us, is Identity (taw<u>h</u>îd), the latter Unification (taw<u>h</u>îd), not in the commonalty's meaning of taw<u>h</u>îd, he honestly says (p. [20]), for them this is one of "the mysteries which we are not at liberty to discuss"--but at the same time not inconsistent With that meaning. What he had in mind was, perhaps, something like this: "I reject the herd's interpretation of taw<u>h</u>îd, the mere declaration-of-the-oneness of Allâh, as a bare truism, miserable in its inadequacy. I likewise reject the other extreme, the pantheist's interpretation of the word as an absolute denial of the actuality of things, or an assertion that things are Allâh. Against them both I assert that Allâh and the Universe constitute a UNITY, but one wherein the Universe is wholly relative to and dependent on Allâh, for existence or nonexistence; preservation or annihilation. All existing things are and must be 'united' to Allâh. But even this must not be declare, openly, for, then, what about Iblîs, Hell, and the Damned? I must not seem to teach 'universalism' any more than pantheism. Allâhu a'lam! "

It therefore seems to the writer that Ghazzâlî's position, which he tortured rather than explained when he tried to describe and illlustrate it, really amounted to nothing more than the inevitable distinction between absolute and relative being; between things when viewed relationally, in their relation to their Author, and things viewed apart from that relation. Neither Author nor Things were to be denied actuality, or reality, as we understand the latter term. As between Allâh and human intelligences he even goes great lengths (in this very treatise of all others) in asserting parallelism and comparability, similarity therefore [1] but between Allâh and all else ONE fundamental all-sufficient difference had to be asserted; namely, ALLAH is self-subsistent, qayyûm; things are not so. This distinction was the minimum one; yet also the maximum, for it preserved at once Creator and created, and gave actuality to each. There is, in truth, a good deal of wilful paradox in the Mishkât, of Oriental hyperbole, of pious highfalutin [2] intended perhaps to scare the "unco" orthodox of the day, to make their flesh creep a little for their health's sake, and to "wake them out of their dogmatic slumbers". For it is in the Mishkât that we find the following words, too, which seem plain and harmless enough: "Being is itself divided into that which has being-in-itself, and that which derives its being from not-itself. The being of this latter is borrowed, having no existence by itself. Nay, if it is regarded in and by itself it is pure not-being. Whatever being

---

[1] And to assert similarity between two things is at once to have asserted two, and a distinction between them. See M, p. [7].
[2] Is not this true for all S̱ûfî writers? Do we not take their language too seriously? It parades as scientific; it is really poetico-rhetorical.]

it has is due to its relation to not-itself, which is not real being at all . . ." In other words, it is by a purely arbitrary mental abstraction that we "regard derived being in and by itself". The impossibility of really effecting this abstraction is precisely what preserves to derived being its measure of actuality --"whatever being it has . . ."[1] To us these last words are a clear concession of reality to conditioned being. It is true Ghazzâlî denies reality to it in the next sentence. But this only shows that when an Oriental talks of "Real" he means what we mean by "Unconditioned", and that when he is thinking of "Conditioned or Relative" he says "Unreal." The matter has become one of terms.

It is impossible to demand more than this from Ghazzâlî as philosopher-theologian. He was, perhaps, not more successful than other eastern theologians in finding a place for the universe, philosophically, with or in Allâh. But has western philosophy been any more successful in finding a place for Allâh, philosophically, with or in the universe?

---

[1] Gh. has no more use for the Noumenon, for the Ding an sich, than had the post-Kantians; though for how different reasons.]

TRANSLATION

[The references in square brackets are to the pages of the Cairo Arabic edition. {these are written in the form [p. 3], to avoid confusion with the footnote indicators.--jbh}]

THE NICHE FOR LIGHTS

(Mishkât al-Anwâr)

Praise to ALLAH! who poureth forth light; and giveth sight; and, from His mysteries' height, removes the veils of night!

And Prayer for MUHAMMED! of all lights the Light; Sire of them that do the right; Beloved of The Sovereign of Might; Evangelist of the forgiven in his sight; to Him devoted quite; to sinner and to infidel the Arm that knows to fight and smile!

You have asked me, dear brother--and may Allâh decree for you the quest of man's chiefest bliss, make you candidate for the Ascent to the highest height anoint your vision with the light of Reality, and purge your inward parts from all that is not the Real!--You have asked me, I say, to communicate to you the mysteries of the Lights Divine, together with the allusions behind the literal meaning of certain texts in the Koran and certain sayings in the Traditions.

And principally this text [1]--

"Allâh is the Light of the Heavens and of the Earth. The similitude of His Light is as it were a Niche wherein is a Lamp: the Lamp within a Glass: the Glass as it were a pearly Star. From a Tree right blessed is it lit, an Olive-tree neither of the East nor of the West, the Oil whereof were well-nigh luminous though Fire touched it not: Light upon Light!

"But as for the Infidels, their deeds are as it were massed Darkness upon some fathomless sea, the which is overwhelmed with billow topped by billow topped by cloud: Darkness on Darkness piled! so that when a man putteth forth his hand he well-nigh can see it not. Yea, the man for whom Allâh doth not cause light, no light at all hath he."

What is the significance of His comparison of LIGHT with Niche, and Glass, and Lamp, and Oil, and Tree?

And this Tradition

"Allâh hath Seventy Thousand Veils of Light and Darkness: were He to withdraw their curtain, then would the splendours of His Aspect [2] surely consume everyone who apprehended Him with his sight."

Such is your request. But in making it you have assayed to climb an arduous ascent, so high that the height thereof cannot be so much as gauged by mortal eyes [p. 3]. You have knocked at a locked door which is only opened to those who know and "are

---

[1] The Light-Verse in S. 24, 35. The Darkness-Verse. which almost immediately follows, and is mentioned in the exposition, has been added.]

[2] Or Countenance; see Introduction, p. 66.

established in knowledge."[1] Moreover, not every mystery is to be laid bare or made plain, but--

"Noble hearts seal mysteries like the tomb."

Or, as one of those who Know has said--

"To divulge the secret of the Godhead is to deny God."

Or, as the Prophet has said--

"There is a knowledge like the form of a hidden thing, known to none save those who know God."

If then these speak of that secret, only the Children of Ignorance will contradict them. And howsoever many these Ignorants be, the Mysteries must from the gaze of sinners be kept inviolate.

But I believe that your heart has been opened by the Light and your consciousness purged of the darkness of Ignorance. I will, therefore, not be so niggardly as to deny you direction to these glorious truths in all their fineness and all their divineness; for the wrong done in keeping Wisdom from her Children is not less than that of yielding her to those who are Strangers to her. As the poet hath it--

"He who bestoweth Knowledge on fools loseth it,
And he who keepeth the deserving from her doeth a wrong."

You must, however, be content with a very summarized explanation of the subject; for the full demonstration of my

---
[1] Cf. S. 3, 6.]

theme would demand a treatment of both its principles and its parts for which my time is at present insufficient, and for which neither my mind nor my energies are free. The keys of all hearts are in the hands of Allah: He opens them when He pleases, as He pleases, and with what {p. 79} He pleases. At this time, then, it shall suffice to open up to you three chapters or parts, whereof the first is as hereunder follows.

PART I.--LIGHT, AND LIGHTS: PRELIMINARY STUDIES

1. "Light" as Physical Light; as the Eye; as the Intelligence

The Real Light is Allâh; and the name "light" is otherwise only predicated metaphorically and conveys no real meaning.

To explain this theme: you must know that the word light is employed with a threefold signification: the first [p. 4] by the Many, the second by the Few, the third by the Fewest of the Few. Then you must know the various grades of light that relate to the two latter classes, and the degrees of the reality appertaining to these grades, in order that it may be disclosed to you, as these grades become clear, that ALLAH is the highest and the ultimate Light: and further, as the reality appertaining to each grade is revealed, that Allâh alone is the Real, the True Light, and beside Him there is no light at all.

Take now the first signification. Here the word light indicates a phenomenon. Now a phenomenon, or appearance, is a relative term, for a thing necessarily appears to, or is concealed from, something other than itself; and thus its appearance and its non-appearance are both relative. Further, its appearance and its nonappearance are relative to perceptive faculties; and of these the most powerful and the most conspicuous, in the opinion of the Many, are the senses, one of which is the sense of sight. Further, things in relation to this sense of sight fall under these categories: (1) that which by itself is not visible, as dark bodies; (2) that which is by itself visible, but cannot make visible anything else, such as luminaries like the stars, and fire before it blazes up; (3) that which is by itself visible, and also makes visible, like the sun and the moon, and fire when it blazes up, and lamps. Now it is in regard to this third category that the name "light" is given: sometimes to that which is effused from these luminaries and falls on the exterior of opaque bodies, as when we say "The earth is lighted up", or "The light of the sun falls on the earth", or "The lamp-light falls on wall or on garment"; and sometimes to the luminaries themselves, because they are self-luminous. In sum, then, light is an expression for that which is by itself visible and [p. 5] makes other things visible, like the sun. This is the definition of, and the reality concerning, light, according to its first signification.

We have seen that the very essence of light is appearance to a percipient; and that perception depends on the existence of two things--light and a seeing eye. For, though light is that which appears and causes-to-appear, it neither appears nor causes-to-appear to the blind. Thus percipient spirit is as important as perceptible light quâ necessary element of perception; nay, 'tis the more important, in that it is the percipient spirit which apprehends and through which apprehension takes place; whereas light is not apprehensive, neither does apprehension takes place through it, but merely when it is present. By the word light, in fact, is more properly understood that visualizing light which we call the eye. Thus men apply the word light to the light of the eye, and say of the weak-sighted that "the light of his eye is weak", and of the blear-eyed that "the light of his vision is impaired," and of the blind that "his light is quenched." Similarly of the pupil of the eye it is said that it concentrates "the light of vision, and strengthens it, the eyelashes being given by the divine wisdom a black colour, and made to compass the eye every way round about, in order to concentrate its "light." And of the white of the eye it is said that it disperses the "light of the eye" and weakens it, so that to look long at a bright white surface, or still more at the sun's light, dazzles "the light of the eye" and effaces it, just as the weak are effaced by the side of the strong. You understand, then, that percipient spirit is called light; and why it is so called; and why it is more properly so called. And this is the second signification, that employed by the Few.

You must know, further, that the light of physical sight is [p. 6] marked by several kinds of defects. It sees others but not itself. Again, it does not see what is very distant, nor what is very near, nor what is behind a veil. It sees the exterior of things only, not their interior; the parts, not the whole; things finite, not things infinite. It makes many mistakes in its seeing, for what is large appears to its vision small; what is far, near; what is at rest, at motion; what is in motion, at rest. Here are seven defects inseparably attached to the physical eye. If, then, there be such an Eye as is free from all these physical defects, would not it, I ask, more properly be given the name of light? Know, then, that there is in the mind of man an eye, characterized by just this perfection--that which is variously called Intelligence, Spirit, Human Soul. But we pass over these terms, for the multiplicity of the terms deludes the man of small intelligence into imagining a corresponding multiplicity of ideas. We mean simply that by which the rational man is distinguished from the infant in arms, from the brute beast, and from the lunatic. Let us call it the Intelligence, following the current terminology. So, then, the intelligence is more properly called Light than is the eye, just because in capacity it transcends these seven defects.

Take the first. The eye does not behold itself, but the intelligence does perceive itself as well as others; and it perceives itself as endowed with knowledge, power, etc., and perceives its own knowledge and perceives its knowledge of its own knowledge, and its know, ledge of its knowledge of its own knowledge, and so on ad infinitum. Now, this is a property which cannot conceivably be attributed to anything which perceives by means of a physical instrument like the eye. Behind this, however, [p. 7] lies a mystery the unfolding of which would take long.

Take, now, the second defect: the eye does not see what is very near to it nor what is very far away from it; but to the intelligence near and far are indifferent. In the twinkling of an eye it ascends to the highest heaven above, in another instant to the confines of earth beneath. Nay, when the facts are realized, intelligence is revealed as transcending the very idea of "far" and "near," which occur between material bodies; these compass not the precincts of its holiness, for it is a pattern or sample of the attributes of Allâh. Now the sample must be commensurate with the original, even though it does not rise to the degree of equality [1] with it. And this may move you to set your mind to work upon the true meaning of the tradition: "Allah created Adam after His own likeness." But I do not think fit at the present time to go more deeply into the same.

The third defect: the eye does not perceive what is behind the veil, but the intelligence moves freely about the Throne, the Sedile, and everything beyond the veil of the Heavens, and likewise about the Host Supernal, and the Realm Celestial, just as much as about its own world, and its propinquate, (that is its own) kingdom. The realities of things stand unveiled to the intelligence. Its only veil is one which it assumes of its own sake, which resembles the veil that the eye assumes of its own accord in the closing of its eyelids. But we shall explain this more fully in the third chapter of this work.

---

[1] Reading ### which both sense and rhyme demand

The fourth defect: the eye perceives only the exterior surfaces of things, but not their interior; may, the mere moulds and forms, not the realities; while intelligence breaks through into the inwardness of things and into their secrets; apprehends the reality of things and their essential spirits; [p. 8] elicits their causes and laws--from what they had origin, how they were created, of how many ideal forms they are composed, what rank of Being they occupy, what is their several relation to all other created things, and much else, the exposition of which would take very long; wherein I think good to be brief.

The fifth: the eye sees only a fraction of what exists, for all concepts, and many percepts, are beyond its vision; neither does it apprehend sounds, nor yet smells, nor tastes, nor sensations of hot and cold, nor the percipient faculties, by which I mean the faculties of hearing, of smelling, of tasting. nay, all the inner psychical qualities are unseen to it, joy, pleasure, displeasure, grief, pain, delight, love, lust, power, will, knowledge, and innumerable other existences. Thus it is narrow in its scope, limited in its field of action, unable to pass the confines of the world of colour and form, which are the grossest of all entities; for natural bodies are in themselves the grossest of the categories of being, and colour and form are the grossest of their properties. But the domain of intelligence is the entirety of existence, for it both apprehends the entities we have enumerated, and has free course among all others beside (and they are the major part), passing upon them judgments that are both certain and true. To it, therefore, are the inward secrets of things manifest, and the hidden forms of things clear. Then tell me by what right the physical eye is given equality with the intelligence in claiming the name of Light? No verily! it is only relatively light; but in relation to the intelligence it is darkness. Sight is but one of the spies of Intelligence [p. 9] who sets it to watch the grossest of his treasures, namely, the treasury of colours and forms; bids it carry reports about the same to its

Lord, who then judges thereof in accordance with the dictates of his penetration and his judgment. Likewise are all the other faculties but Intelligence's spies--imagination, phantasy, thought, memory, recollection; and behind them are servitors and retainers, constrained to his service in this present world of his. These, I say, he constrains, and among these he moves at will, as freely as monarch constrains his vassals to his service, yea, and more freely still. But to expound this would take us long, and we have already treated of it in the book of my Ihyâ` al-`Ulûm, entitled "The Marvels of the Mind".

The sixth: the eye does not see what is infinite. What it sees is the attributes of known bodies, and these can only be conceived as finite. But the intelligence apprehends concepts, and concepts cannot be conceived as finite. True, in respect of the knowledge which has actually been attained, the content actually presented to the intelligence is no more than finite, but potentially it does apprehend that which is infinite. It would take too long to explain this fully, but if you desire an example, here is one from arithmetic. In this science the intelligence apprehends the series of integers, which series is infinite; further, it apprehends the coefficients of two, three, and all the other integers, and to these also no limit can be conceived; and it apprehends all the different relations between numbers, and to these also no limit can be conceived; and finally it apprehends its own knowledge of a thing, and its knowledge of its knowledge of its knowledge of that thing; and so on, potentially, to infinity.

The seventh: the eye apprehends the large as small. It sees the sun the size of a bowl, and the stars like silver-pieces scattered upon a carpet of azure. But intelligence apprehends that the stars [p. 10] and the sun are larger, times upon times, than the earth. To the eye the stars seem to be standing still, and the boy to be getting no taller. But the intelligence sees the boy moving constantly as he grows; the shadow lengthening constantly; and the stars moving every instant, through distances of many miles. As the Prophet said to Gabriel, asking: "Has the sun moved?" And Gabriel. answered: "No--Yes." "How so?" asked he; and the other replied: "Between my saying No and Yes it has moved a distance equal to five hundred years." And so the mistakes of vision are manifold, but the intelligence transcends them all.

Perhaps you will say, we see those who are Possessed of intelligence making mistakes nevertheless, I reply, their imaginative and phantastic faculties often pass judgments and form convictions which they think are the judgments of the intelligence. The error is therefore to be attributed to those lower faculties. See my account of all these faculties in my Mî`âr al-`Ilm and Mahakk al-Nazar. But when the intelligence is separated from the deceptions of the phantasy and the imagination, error on its part is inconceivable; it sees things as they are. This separation is, however, difficult, and only attains perfection after death. Then is error unveiled, and then are mysteries brought to light, and each one meets the weal or the woe which he has already laid up for himself, and "beholds a Book, which reckons each venial and each mortal sin, without omitting a single one".[1] In that hour it shall be said unto him: "We have stripped from thee the Veil that covered thee and thy vision this day is iron."[2] Now that covering Veil is even that of the imagination and the phantasy; and therefore the man who has been deluded by his own fancies, his false beliefs, and his vain imaginations, replies: "Our Lord! We have seen Thee and

---

[1] S. 50, 18
[2] S. 22, 50.]

heard Thee! [p.11] O send us back and we will do good.[1] Verily now we have certain knowledge!"

From all which you understand that the eye may more justly be called Light than the light (so called) which is apprehended by sense; and further that the intelligence should more properly be called Light than the eye. It would be even true to say that between these two there exists so great a difference in value, that we may, nay we must, consider only the INTELLIGENCE as deserving the name Light at all.

2. The Koran as the Sun of the Intelligence

Further you must notice here, that while the intelligence of men does truly see, the things it sees are not all upon the same plane. Its knowledge is in some cases, so to speak, given, that is, present in the intelligence, as in the case of axiomatic truths, e.g. that the same thing cannot be both with and without an origin; or existent and non-existent; or that the same proposition cannot be both true and false; or that the judgment which is true of one thing is true of an identically similar thing; or that, granted the existence of the particular, the existence of the universal must necessarily follow.

For example, granted the existence of black, the existence of "colour" follows; and the same with "man" and "animal"; but the converse does not present itself to the intelligence as necessarily true; for "colour" does not involve "black", nor does "animal" involve "man". And there are many other true propositions, some necessary, some contingent, and some impossible. Other propositions, again, do not find the intelligence invariably with them, when they recur to it, but have to

---

[1] S. 12, 32

shake it up, arouse it, strike flint on steel, in order to elicit its spark. Instances of such propositions are the theorems of speculation, to apprehend which the intelligence has to be aroused by the dialectic (kalâm) of the philosophers. Thus it is when the light of philosophy dawns that man sees actually, after having before seen potentially. Now the greatest [p. 12] of philosophies is the word (kalâm) of Allah in general, and the Koran in particular.

Therefore the verses of the Koran, in relation to intelligence, have the value of sunlight in relation to the eyesight, to wit, it is by this sunlight that the act of seeing is accomplished. And therefore the Koran is most properly of all called Light, just as the light of the sun is called light. The Koran, then, is represented to us by the sun, and the intelligence by the Light of the Eye, and hereby we understand the meaning of the verse, which said: "Believe then on Allâh and His Prophet, and the Light which We caused to descend;"[1] and again: "There hath come a sure proof from your Lord, and We have caused a clear Light to descend."[2]

3. The Worlds Visible and Invisible: with their Lights

You have now realized that there are two kinds of eye, an external and an internal; that the former belongs to one world, the World of Sense, and that internal vision belongs to another world altogether, the World of the Realm Celestial; and that each of these two eyes has a sun and a light whereby its seeing is perfected; and that one of these suns is external, the other internal, the former belonging to the seen world, viz. the sun, which is an object of sense perception, and the other internal, belonging to the world of the Realm Celestial, viz. the Koran,

---

[1] S. 64, 8.
[2] S. 4, 173.

and other inspired books of Allah. If, then, this has been disclosed to you thoroughly and entirely, then one of the doors of this Realm Celestial has been opened unto you. In that world there are marvels, in comparison with which this world of sight is utterly condemned. He who never fares to that world, but allows the limitations of life in this lower world of sense to settle upon him, is still a(brute beast, an excommunicate from that which constitutes us men; gone astray is he more than any brute beast, for to the brute are not vouched the wings of flight, on which to fly away unto that invisible world. "Such men," the Koran says, "are cattle, nay, are yet further astray!"[1] [p. 13] As the rind is to the fruit; as the mould or the form in relation to the spirit, as darkness in relation to light; as infernal to supernal; so is this World of Sense in relation to the world of the Realm Celestial. For this reason the latter is called the World Supernal or the World of Spirit, or the World of Light, in contrast with the World Beneath, the World of Matter and of Darkness. But do not imagine that I mean by the World Supernal the World of the [Seven] Heavens, though they are "above" in respect of part of our world of sense-perception. These heavens are equally present to our apprehension, and that of the lower animals. But a man finds the doors of the Realm Celestial closed to him, neither does he become of or belonging to that Realm unless "this earth to him be changed into that which is not earth, and likewise the heavens"[2]; unless, in short, all that comes within the ken of his sense and his imagination, including the visible heavens, cause to be his earth, and his heaven come to be all that transcends his sense. This is the first Ascension for every Pilgrim, who has set out on his Progress to approach the Presence Dominical. Thus mankind was consigned back to the lowest of the low, and must thence rise to the world of highest

---

[1] S. 7, 178.
[2] S. 14, 48.

height. Not so is it with the Angels; for they are part of the World of the Realm Celestial, floating ever in the Presence of the Transcen-dence, whence, they gaze down upon our World Inferior. Thereof spoke the Prophet in the Tradition: "Allâh created the creation in darkness, then sent an effusion of His light upon it," and "Allâh hath Angels, beings who know the works often better than they know them themselves." Now the Prophets, when their ascents reached unto the World of the Realm Celestial, attained the uttermost goal, and from thence looked down upon a totality of the World Invisible; for he who is in the World of the Realm Celestial is with Allâh, and hath the keys [p. 14] of the Unseen. I mean that from where he is the causes of existing things descend into the World of Sense; for the world of sense is one of the effects of yonder world of cause, resulting from it just as the shadow results from a body, or as fruit from that which fructuates, or as the effect from a cause. Now the key to this knowledge of the effect is sought and found in the cause. And for this reason the World of Sense is a type of the World of the Realm Celestial, as will appear when we explain the NICHE, the LAMP, and the TREE. For the thine, compared is in some sort parallel, and bears resemblance, to the thing compared therewith, whether that resemblance be remote or near: a matter, again, which is unfathomably deep, so that whoever has scanned its inner meaning had revealed to him the verities of the types in the Koran by an easy way.

I said that everything that sees self and not-self deserves more properly the name of Light, while that which adds to these two functions the function of making the not-self visible, still more properly deserves the name of Light than that which has no effect whatever beyond itself. This is the light which merits the name of "Lamp Illuminant",[1] because its light is effused upon the not-self. Now this is the property of the transcendental prophetic spirit, for through its means are effused the illuminations of the sciences upon the created world. Thus is explained the name given by Allâh to Mohammed, "Illuminant."[2] Now all the Prophets are Lamps, and so are the Learned-but the difference between them is incalculable.

4. These Lights as Lamps Terrestrial and Celestial: with their Order and Grades

If it is proper to call that from which the light of vision emanates a "Lamp Illuminant", then that from which the Lamp is itself lit may [p. 15] meetly be symbolized by Fire. Now all these Lamps Terrestrial were originally lit from the Light Supernal alone; and of the transcendental Spirit of prophecy it is written that "Its oil were well-nigh luminous though fire touched it not"; but becomes "very light upon light" when touched by that Fire.[3] Assuredly, then, the kindling source of those Spirits Terrestrial is the divine Spirits Supernal, described by Ali and Ibn Abbas, when they said that "Allâh hath an Angel with countenances seventy thousand, to each countenance seventy thousand mouths, in each mouth seventy thousand tongues wherewith he laudeth God most High". This is he who is contrasted with all the angelic host, in the words: "On the day whereon THE SPIRIT ariseth and the Angels, rank on rank."[4] These Spirits Celestial, then, if they be considered as the kindling-source of the Lamps

---

[1] S. 33, 46.
[2] S. 46, 33
[3] S. 24, 35; see p. [45] of translation.
[4] S. 28, 78.]

Terrestrial, can be compared alone with "Fire".[1] And that kindling is not perceived save "on the Mountain's side"[2]

Let us now take these Lights Celestial from which are lit the Lamps Terrestrial, and let us rank them in the order in which they themselves are kindled, the one from the other. Then the nearest to the fountain-head will be of all others the worthiest of the name of Light for he is the highest in order and rank. Now the analogy for this graded order in the world of sense can only be seized by one who sees the light of the moon coming through the window of a house, falling on a mirror fixed upon a wall, which reflects that light on to another wall, whence it in turn is reflected on the floor, so that the floor becomes illuminated therefrom. The light upon the floor is owed to that upon the wall, and the light on the wail to that in the mirror, and the light in the mirror to that from the moon, and the light in the moon to that from the sun, [16] for it is the sun that radiates its light upon the moon. Thus these four lights are ranged one above the other, each one more perfect than the other; and each one has a certain rank and a proper degree which it never passes beyond. I would have you know, then, that it has been revealed to the men of Insight that even so are the Lights of the Realm Celestial ranged in an order; and that the highest is the one who is nearest to the Ultimate Light. It may well be, then, that the rank of Seraphiel is above the rank of Gabriel; and that among them is that Nighest to Allâh, he whose rank comes nighest to the Presence Dominical which is the Fountain-head of all these lights; and that among these is a Nighest to Man, and that between these two are grades innumerable, whereof all that is known is that they are many, and that they are ordered in rank and grade, and that as they have described themselves, so they are indeed--"Not one of us

---

[1] S. 28, 29.
[2] S. 28, 29: also 19, 53.]

but has his determined place and standing,"[1] and "We are verily the ranked ones; we are they in whose mouth is Praise."[2]

5. The Source of all these Grades of Light: ALLAH

The next thing I would have you know is that these degrees of light do not ascend in an infinite series, but rise to a final Fountain-head who is Light in and by Himself, upon Whom comes no light from any external source, and from Whom every light is effused according to, its order and grade. Ask yourself, now whether the name Light is more due to that which is illumined and borrows its light from an external source; or that which in itself is luminous, illuminating all else beside? I do not believe that you can fail to see the true answer, and thus conclude that the name light is most of all due to this LIGHT SUPERNAL, above Whom there is no light at all, and from Whom light descends upon all other things.

Nay, I do not hesitate to say boldly that the term "light" as applied to aught else than this primary light is purely metaphorical; for all [p. 17] others, if considered in themselves, have, in themselves and by themselves, no light at all. Their light is borrowed from a foreign source; which borrowed illumination has not any support in itself, only in something not-itself. But to call the borrower by the same name as the lender is mere metaphor. Think you that the man who borrows riding-habit, saddle, horse, or other riding beast, and mounts the same when and as the lender appoints, is actually, or only metaphorically, rich? Or is it the lender who alone is rich? The latter, assuredly! The borrower remains in himself as poor as ever, and only of him who made the loan and exacts its return can richness be predicated--him who gave and can take away. Therefore, the

---
[1] S. 37, 164-7
[2] S. 37, 164-7

Real Light is He in Whose hand lies creation and its destinies; He who first gives the light and afterwards sustains it. He shares with no other the reality of this name, nor the full title to the same; save in so far as He calls some other by that name, deigns to call him by it in the same way as a Liege-Lord deigns to give his vassal a fief, and therewith bestows on him the title of lord. Now when that vassal realizes the truth, he understands that both he and his are the property of his Liege, and of Him alone, a property shared by Him with no partner in the world.

You now know that Light is summed up in appearing and manifesting, and you have ascertained the various gradations of the same. You must further know that there is no darkness so intense as the darkness of No-being. For [1] a dark thing is called "dark" simply because it cannot appear to anyone's vision; it never comes to exist for sight, though it does exist in itself. But that which has no existence for others nor for itself is assuredly the very extreme of darkness. In contrast with it is Being, which is, therefore, Light; for unless a thing is manifest in itself, [p. 18] it is not manifest to others. Moreover, Being is itself divided into that which has being in itself, and that which derives its being from not-itself. That being of this latter is borrowed, having no existence by itself. Nay, if it is regarded in and by itself, it is pure not-being. Whatever being it has is due to its relation to a not-itself; and this is not real being at all, as you learned from my parable of the Rich and the Borrowed Garment. Therefore, Real Being is Allâh most High, even as Real Light is likewise Allâh.

6. The Mystic Verity of Verities

It is from this starting-point that Allâh's gnostics rise from metaphors to realities, as one climbs from the lowlands to the mountains; and at the end of their Ascent see, as with the direct

---

[1] Reading ### for ###

sight of eye-witnesses, that there is nothing in existence save Allâh alone, and that "everything perisheth except His Countenance, His Aspect"[1] (wajh); not that [2] it perisheth at some particular moment, but rather it is sempiternally a perishing thing, since it cannot be conceived except as perishing. For each several thing other than Allâh is, when considered in and by itself, pure not-being; and if considered from the "aspect" (wajh) to which existence flows from the Prime Reality, it is viewed as existing, but not in itself, solely from the "aspect" which accompanies Him Who gives it existence. Therefore, the God-aspect is the sole thing in existence. For everything has two aspects, an aspect to itself and an aspect to its Lord: in respect of the first, it is Not-being; but in respect of the God-aspect, it is Being. Therefore there is no Existent except God and the God-aspect, and therefore all things are perishing except the God-aspect from and to all eternity. These gnostics, therefore, have no need to await the arising of the Last Uprising in order to hear the Creator proclaim, "To whom is the power this day? To ALLAH! the One, the Not-to-be-withstood"[3]; [p. 19] for that summons is pealing in their ears always and for ever. Neither do they understand by the cry "Allah is most great" (Allâhu akbar) that He is only "greater" than others. God forbid! For in all existence there is beside Him none for Him to exceed in greatness. No other attains so much as to the degree of co-existence, or of sequent existence, nay of existence at all, except from the Aspect that accompanies Him. All existence is, exclusively, His Aspect. Now it is impossible that He should be "greater"' than His own Aspect. The meaning is rather that he is too absolutely Great to be called Greater, or Most Great, by way of relation or comparison--too Great for anyone, whether Prophet or Angel, to grasp the real nature of His Greatness. For

---

[1] S. 88, 28
[2] Reading ###.]
[3] S. 16, 40

none knows Allah with a real knowledge but He Himself; for every, known falls necessarily under the sway and within the province of the Knower; a state: which is the very negation of all Majesty, all "Greatness". The full proof whereof I have given in my al-Maqsad al-Asnâ fî ma`ânî asmâ'i llâhi-l Husnâ.

These gnostics, on their return from their Ascent into the heaven of Reality, confess with one voice that they saw nought existent there save the One Real. Some of them, however, arrived at this scientifically, and others experimentally and subjectively. From these last the plurality of things fell away in its entirety. They were drowned in the absolute Unitude, and their intelligences were lost in Its abyss. Therein became they as dumbfounded things. No capacity remained within them save to recall ALLAH; yea, not so much as the capacity to recall their own selves. So there remained nothing with them save ALLAH. They became drunken with a drunkenness wherein the sway of their own intelligence disappeared; so that one [1] exclaimed, "I am The ONE REAL!" and another, "Glory be to ME! How great is MY glory! [2] and another, "Within this robe is nought but Allâh!"[3] ... But the words of

Lovers Passionate in their intoxication and ecstasy [p. 20] must be hidden away and not spoken of . . . Then when that drunkenness abated and they came again under the sway of the intelligence, which is Allâh's balance-scale upon earth, they knew that that had not been actual Identity, but only something resembling Identity; as in those words of the Lover at the height of his passion:--

"I am He whom I love and He whom I love is I;

---

[1] Al-Hallâj.
[2] Abû Yazîd al-Bistâmî. See Massignon's Hallâj, p. 513.]
[3] Abû Yazîd al-Bistâmî. See Massignon's Hallâj, p. 513.]

We are two spirits immanent in one body."[1]

For it is possible for a man who has never seen a mirror in his life, to be confronted suddenly by a mirror, to look into it, and to think that the form which he sees in the mirror is the form of the mirror itself, "identical" with it. Another might see wine in a glass, and think that the wine is just the stain of the glass. And if that thought becomes with him use and wont, like a fixed idea with him, it absorbs him wholly, so that he sings:--

"The glass is thin, the wine is clear!
The twain are alike, the matter is perplexed:

For 'tis as though there were wine and no wineglass there,
Or as though mere were wine-glass and nought of wine!"

He there is a difference between saying, "The wine is the wine-glass," and saying, "'tis as though it were the wine-glass." Now, when this state prevails, it is called in relation to him who experiences it, Extinction, nay, Extinction of Extinction, for the soul has become extinct to itself, extinct to its own extinction; for it becomes unconscious of itself and unconscious of its own unconsciousness, since, were it conscious of its own unconsciousness, it would be conscious of itself. In relation to the man immersed in this state, the state is called, in the language of metaphor, "Identity"; in the language of reality, "Unification." And beneath these verities also lie mysteries which we are not at liberty to discuss.

7. The "God-Aspect": an "advanced" Explanation of the Relation of these Lights to ALLAH

---

[1] By al-Ḥallâj

It may be that you desire greatly to know the aspect (wajh) [p. 21] whereby Allâh's light is related to the heavens and the earth, or rather the aspect whereby He is in Himself the Light of heavens and earth. And this shall assuredly not be denied you, now that you know that Allâh is Light, and that beside Him there is no light, and that He is every light, and that He is the universal light: since light is an expression for that by which things are revealed; or, higher still, that by and for which they are revealed; yea, and higher still, that by, for, and from which they are revealed: and now that, you know, too that, of everything called light, only that by, for, and from which things are revealed is real--that Light beyond which there is no light to kindle and feed its flame, for It is kindled and fed in itself, from Itself, and for Itself, and from no other source at all. Such a conception, such a description, you are now assured, can be applied to the Great Primary, alone. You are also assured that the heavens and the earth are filled with light appertaining to those two fundamental light-planes, our Sight and our Insight; by which I mean our senses and our intelligence. The first kind of light is what we see in the heavens--sun and moon and stars; and what we see in earth--that is, the rays which are poured over the whole face of the earth, making visible all the different colours and hues, especially in the season of spring; and over all animals and plants and things, in all their states: for without these rays no colour would appear or even exist. Moreover, every shape and size which is visible to perception is apprehended in consequence of colour, and it is impossible to conceive of apprehending them without colour. As for the other ideal, intelligential Lights, the World Supernal is filled with them--to wit, the angelic substance; and the World Inferior is also full of them--[p. 22] to wit, animal life and human life successively. The order of the World Inferior is manifested by means of this inferior human light; while the order of the World Supernal is manifested by means of that angelical light. This is the order alluded to in the passage in the Koran, "He it is Who has formed you from the earth, and hath peopled it with you, that He might call you Successors upon the earth" . . . and "Maketh you Successors on the earth," and "Verily I have set in the earth a Successor" (Khalîfa).[1]

Thus you see that the whole world is all filled with the external lights of perception, and the internal lights of intelligence; also that the lower lights are effused or emanate the one from the other, as light emanates or is effused from a lamp; while the Lamp itself is the transcendental Light of Prophecy; and that, the transcendental Spirits of Prophesy are lit from the Spirit Supernal, as the lamp is lit from fire; and that the Supernals are lit the one from the other; and that their order is one of ascending grades: further, that these all rise to the Light of Lights, the Origin and Fountainhead of lights, and that is ALLAH, only and alone; and that all other lights are borrowed from Him, and that His alone is real light; and that everything is from His light, nay, He is everything, nay, HE IS THAT HE is, none but He has ipseity or heity at all, save by metaphor. Therefore there is no light but He, while all other lights are only lights from the Aspect which accompanies Him, not from themselves. Thus the aspect and face of everything faces to Him and turns in His direction; and "whithersoever they turn themselves there is the Face of Allâh [2] So, then, there is no divinity but HE; for "divinity" is an expression by which is connoted that towards which all faces are directed [3] in worship and in confession--that He is Deity; but which I mean the faces of the hearts of men, for they verily are lights and spirits. Nay, more, just as "there is no deity

---

[1] S. 61, 11; 55, 24; 62, 27; 30, 2. Cf. Mishkât, p.[34].
[2] S. 2. 115, see 144, 149, 150.
[3] Gh.'s piece of amateur etymology here, by which he appears to derive the root 'lh ("god") from the root wty ("turn"), is about as absurd as my attempt to suggest it in the English.]

but He," so there is no heity but He, [p. 23] for "he" is an expression for something which one can indicate; but in every and any case we can but indicate Him. Every time you indicate anything, your indication is in reality, to Him, even though through your ignorance of the truth of truths which we have mentioned you know it not. Just as one cannot point to, indicate, sunlight but only the sun, so the relation of the sum of things to Allâh is, in the visible analogue, as the relation of light to the sun. Therefore "There is no deity but ALLAH" is the Many's declaration of Unity: that of the Few is "There is no he but HE"; the former is more general, but the latter is more particular, more comprehensive, more exact, and more apt to give him who declares it entrance into the pure and absolute Oneness and Onliness. This kingdom of the One-and-Onliness is the ultimate point of mortals' Ascent: there is no ascending stage beyond it; for "ascending" involves plurality, being a sort of relatively involving two stages, an ascent from and an ascent to. But when Plurality has been eliminated, Unity is established, relation is effaced, all indication from "here" to "there" falls away, and there remains neither height nor depth, nor anyone to fare up or down. The upward Progress, the Ascent of the soul, then becomes impossible, for there is no height beyond the Highest, no plurality alongside of the One, and, now that plurality has terminated, no Ascent for the soul. If there be, indeed, any change, it is by way of the "Descent into the Lowest Heaven", the radiation from above downwards; for the Highest, though It may have mo higher, has a lower. This is the goal of goals, the last object of spiritual search, known of him who knows it, denied by him who is ignorant of it. It belongs to that knowledge which is according to the form of the hidden thing, and which no one knoweth save the Learned [1] is Allah. If, therefore, they utter it, it is only denied by the Ignorant of Him.

---

[1] Cf. S. 3, 7.

There is no improbability in the explanation given by these Learned to this "Descent into the Lowest Heaven", [p. 24] namely, that it is the descent of an Angel; though one of those Gnostics [1] has, indeed, fancied a less probable explanation. He, immersed as he was in the divine One-and-Onliness, said that Allah has "a descent into the lowest heaven", and that this descent is His descent, in order to use physical senses, and to set in motion bodily limbs; and that He is the one indicated in the Tradition in which the Prophet says, "I have become His hearing whereby He heareth, His vision whereby He seeth, His tongue wherewith He speaketh."[2] Now if the Prophet was Allah's hearing and vision and tongue, then Allah and He alone is the Hearer, the Seer, the Speaker; and He is the one indicated in His own word to Moses, "I was sick, and thou visitedst Me not.[3] According to this, the bodily movements of this Confessor of the divine Unity are from the lowest heaven; his sensation from a heaven next above; and his intelligence from the heaven next above that. From that heaven of the intelligence he fares upward to the limit of the Ascension of created things, the kingdom of the One-and-Onliness, a sevenfold way; thereafter "settleth he himself on the throne" of the divine Unity, and therefrom "taketh command"[4] throughout his storied heavens. Well might one, in looking upon such an one, apply to him the saying, "Allah created Adam after the image of the Merciful One"; until, after contemplating that word more deeply, he becomes aware that it has an interpretation like those other words, "I am the ONE REAL," "Glory be to

---

[1] Al-Hallâjj.
[2] A saying reported by Ibn Adham, d. 170.]
[3] See St, Matt. xxv.
[4] Ar. al amr. See on p. [55], Introduction, pp. 32-40. Or, "controlleth things." And see S, 32, 5.

ME![1] or those sayings of the Prophet, that Allah said, "I was sick and thou visitedst Me not," and "I am His hearing, and His vision; and His tongue". But I see fit now to draw rein in this exposition, for I think that you cannot hear more of this sort than the amount which I have now communicated.

8. The Relation of these Lights to ALLAH: Simpler Illustrations and Explanations

It may well be that you will not rise to the height of these words, for all your pains; it may be that for all your pains you will come short of it after all. Here, then, is something that lies nearer your understanding, and nearer your weakness. The meaning of the doctrine that Allah is [p. 25] the Light of Heavens and Earth may be understood in relation to phenomenal, visible light. When you see hues of spring-the tender green, for example-in the full light of day, you entertain no doubt but that you are looking on colours, and very likely you suppose that you are looking on nothing else alongside of them. As though you should say, "I see nothing alongside of the green." Many have in fact, obstinately maintained this. They have asserted that light is a meaningless term, and that there is nothing but colour with the colours. Thus they denied the existence of the light, although it was the most manifest of all things--how should it not be so, considering that through it alone all things become manifest?, for it is the thing that is itself visible and makes visible, as we said before. But, when the sun sank, and heaven's lamp disappeared from sight, and night's shadow fell, then apprehended these men the existence of an essential difference between inherent shadow and inherent light; and they confessed that light is a form that lies behind all colour, and is apprehended with colour, insomuch that, so to speak, through its intense union with the colours it is not

---

[1] M, p. [19].

apprehended, and through its intense obviousness it is invisible. And it may be that this very intensity is the direct cause of its invisibility, for things that go beyond one extreme pass over to the extreme opposite.

If this is clear to you, you must further know that those endowed with this Insight never saw a single object without seeing Allah along with it. It may be that one of them went further than this and said, "I have never seen a single object, but I first saw Allah"; for some of, them only see objects through and in Allah, while others first see objects and then see Allah in and through those objects. It is to the first class that the Koran alludes to in the words, "Doth it not suffice that My Lord seeth all?" [1] and to the second in the words, "We shall shew them our signs in all the world and in themselves." For the first class [p. 26] have the direct intuition of Allah, and the second infer Him from His works. The former is the rank of the Saint-Friends of God, the latter of the Learned "who are established in knowledge"[2] After these two grades there remains nothing except that of the careless, on whose faces is the veil.

Thus you see that just as everything is manifest to man's Sight by means of light, so everything is manifest to man's Insight by means of Allah; for He is with everything every moment and by Him does everything appear. But here the analogy ceases, and we have a radical difference; namely, that phenomenal light can be conceived of as disappearing with the sinking of the sun, and as assuming a veil in order that shadow may appear: while the divine light, which is the condition of all appearance, cannot be conceived as disappearing. That sun can never set! It abides for ever with all things. Thus the method of difference (as a method for the demonstration of the Existence of God from His works)

---

[1] S. 41, 53.
[2] S. 3, 6.

is not at our disposal. Were the appearance of Allah conceivable, heaven and earth would fall to ruin, and thence, through difference, would be apprehended an effect which would simultaneously compel the recognition of the Cause whereby all things appeared. But, as it is, all Nature remains the same and invariable to our sight because of the unity of its Creator, for "all things are singing His praise" [1] (not some things) at all times (not sometimes); and thus the method of difference is eliminated, and the way to the knowledge of God is obscured. For the most manifest way to the knowledge of things is by their contraries: the thing that possesses no contrary and no opposite, its features being always exactly alike when you are looking at it, will very likely elude your notice altogether. In this case its obscureness results from its very obviousness, and its elusiveness from the very radiance of its brightness. Then glory to Him who hides Himself from His own creation by His utter manifestness, and is veiled from their gaze through the very effulgence of His own light!

But it may be that not even this teaching is intelligible to some limited intelligences, [27] who from our statement (that "Allah is with, everything", as the light is with everything) will understand that He is in every place. Too high and holy is He to be related to place! So far from starting this vein imagining, we assert to you that He is prior to everything, and above everything, and that He makes everything manifest. Now manifester is inseparable from, manifested, subjectively, in the cognition of the thinker; and this is what we mean by saying. that Allah accompanies or is "with" everything. You know, further, that manifester is prior to, and above, manifested, though He be "with" it; but he is "with" it from one aspect, and "above" it from another. You are not to suppose, therefore, that there is here any contradiction. Or, consider, how in the world of sense,

---

[1] See S. 17, 44

which is the highest to which your knowledge can rise, the motion of your hands goes "with" the motion of its shadow, and yet is prior to it as well. And whoever has not wit enough to see this, ought to abandon these researches altogether; for

"To every science its own people;
And each man finds easy that for which he has been created apt."

PART II.--THE SCIENCE OF SYMBOLISM

PROLEGOMENA TO THE EXPLANATION OF THE SYMBOLISM OF THE NICHE, THE LAMP, THE GLASS, THE TREE, THE OIL, AND THE FIRE

THE exposition of this symbolism involves, first of all, two cardinal considerations, which afford limitless scope for investigation, but to which I shall merely allude very briefly here.

First, the science and method of symbolism; the way in which the spirit of the ideal form [1] is captured by the mould of the symbol; the mutual relationship of the two; the inner nature of this correspondence between the world of Sense (which supplies the clay of the moulds, the material of the symbolism) and the world of the Realm Supernal from which the Ideas descend. [2]

Second, the gradations of the several spirits of our mortal clay, and the degree [p. 28] of light possessed by each. For we treat of this latter symbolism in order to explain the former.

(i) THE OUTWARD AND THE INWARD IN SYMBOLISM: TYPE AND ANTITYPE

---

[1] Or Idea = in practically the Platonic sense.]
[2] (By Ghazzâlî.) In this Light-Verse, in Ibn Mas'ûd's reading, the words "in the heart of the believer, "follow the words "of His light". And Ubayy b. Ka`b's instead of "the similitude of His light", has "the similitude of the light of the heart of him who believes is like". etc.]

The world is Two Worlds, spiritual and material, or, if you will, a World Sensual and a World Intelligential; or again, if you will, a World Supernal and a World Inferior. All these expressions are near each other, and the difference between them is merely one of viewpoint. If you regard the two worlds in themselves, you use the first expression; if in respect of the organ which apprehends them, the second; if in respect of their mutual relationship, the third. You may, perhaps, also term them the World of Dominance and Sense-perception, and, the World of the Unseen and the Realm Supernal. It were no marvel if the students of the realities underlying the terminology were puzzled by the multiplicity of these terms, and imagined a corresponding multiplicity of ideas. But he to whom the realities beneath the terms are disclosed makes the ideas primary and the terms secondary: while inferior minds take the opposite course. To them the term is the source from which the reality proceeds. We have an allusion to these two types of mind in the Koran, "Whether is the more rightly guided, he who walks with his face bent down, or he who walks in a straight Way, erect? [1]

1. The two Worlds: their types and antitypes

Such is the idea of the Two Worlds. And the next thing for you to know is, that the supernal world of "the Realm" is a world invisible to the majority of men; and the world of our senses is the world of perception, because it is perceived of all. This World Sensual is the point from which we ascend to [p. 29] the world Intelligential: and, but for this connexion between the two, and their reciprocal relationship, the way upward to the higher sphere would be barred. And were this upward was impossible, then would the Progress to the Presence Dominical and the near approach to Allah be impossible too. For no man

---

[1] S. 67, 22.]

shall approach near unto Allah, unless his foot stand at the very centre of the Fold of the Divine Holiness. Now by this World of the "Divine Holiness" we mean the world that transcends the apprehension of the senses and the imagination. And it is in respect of the law of that world--the law that the soul which is a stranger to it neither goeth out therefrom, nor entereth therein--that we call it the Fold of the Divine Holiness and Transcendence. And the human spirit, which is the channel of the manifestations of the Transcendence, may be perhaps called "the Holy Valley" [1]

Again, this Fold comprises lesser folds, some of which penetrate more deeply than others into the ideas of the Divine Holiness. But the term Fold embraces all the gradations of the lesser ones; for you must not suppose that these terms are enigmas, unintelligible to men of Insight. But I cannot pursue the subject further, for I see that my preoccupation with citing and explaining all this terminology is turning me from my theme. It is for you to apply yourself now to the study of the terms.

To return to the subject we were discussing: the visible world is, as we said, the point of departure up to We world of the Realm Supernal; and the "Pilgrim's Progress of the Straight Way" [2] is an expression for that upward course, which may also be expressed by "The Faith," "the Mansions of Right Guidance." Were there no relation between the two worlds, no inter-connexion at all, then all upward progress would be inconceivable from one to the other. Therefore, the divine mercy gave to the World Visible a correspondence with the World of the Realm Supernal, and for this reason there is not a single thing in this world of sense that is not a symbol of something in yonder one. It may

---

[1] S. 20, 12.]
[2] See S. 1, 4.

well hap that some one thing in this world may symbolize several things in the World of the Realm Supernal, and equally well that some one thing in the latter may have several symbols [p. 30] in the World Visible. We call a thing typical or symbolic when it resembles and corresponds to its antitype under some aspect.

A complete enumeration of these symbols would involve our exhausting the whole of the existing things in both of the Two Worlds! Such a task our mortal powers can never fulfil; or human faculties have not sufficed to comprehend it in the past; and with our little lives we cannot expound it fully in the present. The utmost I can do is to explain to you a single example. The greater may then be inferred from the less; for the door of research into the mysteries of this knowledge will then lie open to you.

2. An Example of Symbolism, from the Story of Abraham in the Koran

Listen now. If the World of the Realm Supernal contains Light-substances, high and lofty, called "Angels", from which substances the various lights are effused upon the various mortal spirits, and by reason of which these angels are called "lords," then is Allah "Lord of lords," and these lords will have differing, grades of luminousness. The symbols, then, of these in the visible world will be, preeminently, the Sun, the Moon, and the Stars. And the Pilgrim of the Way rises first of all to a degree corres-ponding to that of a star. The effulgence of that star's light appears to him. It is disclosed to him that the entire world beneath adores its influence and the effulgence of its light. And so, because of the very beauty and superbness of the thing, he is made aware of something which cries aloud saying, "This is my Lord?"[1] He passes on; and as he becomes conscious of the light-degree next above it, namely, that symbolized by the moon, lo! in the aerial canopy he beholds that star set, to wit, in comparison with its superior; and he saith, "Nought that setteth do I adore!" And so he rises till he arrives at last at the degree symbolized by the sun. This, again, he sees is greater and higher than the former, but nevertheless admits of comparison therewith, in, virtue of a relationship between the two. [31] But to bear relationship to what is imperfect carries with it imperfection--the "setting" of our allegory. And by reason thereof he saith: "I have turned my face unto That Who made the heavens and the earth! I am a true believer, and, not of those who associate other gods with Allah!" Now what is meant to be conveyed by this "THAT WHO" is the vaguest kind of indication, destitute of all relation or comparison. For, were anyone to ask, "What is the symbol comparable with or corresponding to this That?" no answer to the question could be conceived. Now He Who transcends all relations is ALLAH, the ONE REALITY. Thus, when certain Arabs once asked the Apostle of God, "To what may we relate Allah?" this reply was revealed, "Say, He, Allah is one! His days are neither ended nor begun; neither is He a father nor a son; and none is like unto Him, no not one"[2]; the meaning of which verse is simply that He transcends relation. Again, when Pharaoh said to Moses: "What, pray, is the Lord of the Universe?" as though demanding to know His essence, Moses, in his reply, merely indicated His works, because these were clearer to the mind of his interroga-

---

[1] See for this whole passage S. 6, 75-8.]
[2] S. 112

tor; and answered, "The Lord of the heavens and the earth."[1] But Pharaoh said to his courtiers, "Ha! marked ye that!" as though objecting to Moses' evasion of his demand to be told Allah's essential nature. Then Moses said, "Your Lord, and your first fathers' Lord." Pharaoh then set him down as insane. He had demanded an analogue, for the description of the divine Essence, and Moses replied to him from His works. And so Pharaoh said, "Your prophet who has been sent you is insane."

3. Fundamental Examples of Symbolism especially from the Story of Moses in the Koran

Let us now return to the pattern we selected for illustrating the symbolic method. The science of the Interpretation of Visions determines for us the value of each kind of symbol; for "Vision is a part of Prophecy." It is clear, is it not, that the sun, when seen in a vision must be interpreted by a Sovereign Monarch, because of their mutual resemblance and their share in a common spiritual idea, to wit, sovereignty over all, and the emanation or effusion of influence and light on to all. The antitype of the moon will be that Sovereign's Minister; for it is through the moon that the sun sheds his light on the world in its own absence; and even so, it is through his own Minister that the Sovereign [p. 32] makes his influence felt by subjects who never beheld the royal person. Again, the dreamer who sees himself with a ring on his finger with which he seals the mouths of men and the secrets of women, is told that the sign means the early Call to Prayer in the month of Ramadan[2]. Again, for one who sees himself pouring olive oil into an olive-tree the interpretation is that the slave-girl he has wedded is his mother,

---

[1] For this passage see S. 26, 24-7, and for the whole thought--compare pp. [54, 55]

[2] Because after the idhân, just before morning, food and sexual intercourse are fasted from till the next sunset.]

unrecognized by him. But it is impossible to exhaust the different ways by which symbols of this description may be interpreted, and I cannot set myself the task of enumerating them. I can merely say that just as certain beings of the Spirit-World Supernal are symbolized by Sun, Moon and Stars, others may be typified by different symbols. when the Point of connexion is some characteristic other than light.

For example, if among those beings of that Spirit-World there be something that is fixed and unchangeable; great and never diminishing; from which the waters of knowledge, the excellencies of revelations, issue into the heart, even as waters well out into a valley; It would be symbolized by the Mountain.[1] Further, if the beings that are the recipients of those excellencies are of diverse grades, they would be symbolized by the Valley; and if those excellencies, on reaching the hearts of men, pass from heart to heart, these hearts are also symbolized by Valleys.[2] The head of the Valley will represent the hearts of Prophet, Saint, and Doctor, followed by those who come after them. So, then, if these valleys are lower than the first one, and are watered from it, then that first one will certainly be the "Right" Valley,[3] because of its signal rightness [4]and superiority. And finally will come the lowest valley which receives its water from the last and lowest level of that "Right" Valley, and is accordingly watered from "the margin of the Right Valley[5] not [p. 33] from its deepest part and centre.

---

[1] S. 28, 29. 46.
[2] S. 13, 18.
[3] S. 28, 30. See S. 19, 53, and 20, 82
[4] Ghazzâlî here plays on the word ayman, the root of which means dexter or felix.
[5] S. 28, 30.

But if the spirit of a prophet is typified by a lighted Lamp, lit by means of Inspiration ("We have inspired thee with [a] Spirit from Our power"), [1] then the symbol of the source of that kindling is Fire. If some of those who derive knowledge from the prophets live by a merely traditional acceptance of what they are told, and others by a gift of insight, then the symbol for the former, who investigate nothing, is a Fire-brand or a Torch or a Meteor; while the man of spiritual experience, who has therefore something in some sort common with the prophets, is accordingly symbolized by the Warming of Fire, for a man is not warmed by hearing about fire but by being close to it.

If the first stage of prophets is their translation into the World of Holy Transcendence away from the disturbances of senses and imagination, that stage is symbolized by "the Holy Valley".[2] And if the Holy Valley may not be trodden save after the doffing of the Two Worlds (that is, this world and the world beyond) and the soul's turning of her face towards the One Real (for this world and the world beyond are co-relatives and both are accidentia of the human light-substance, and can be doffed at one time and donned at another), then the symbol of the putting-off of these Two Worlds is the doffing of his two sandals by the pilgrim to Mekka [3] what time he changes his worldly garments for the pilgrim's robe and faces towards the holy Kaaba.

Nay, but let us now translate ourselves to the Presence Dominical once more, and speak of its symbols. If that Presence hath something whereby the several divine sciences are engraven on the tablets of hearts susceptible to them, that

---

[1] S. 42, 52.]
[2] S. 20, and 79, 16.
[3] S. 20, 12.

something will be symbolized by the Pen.[1] That Within those hearts whereon those things are engraved will be typified by the Tablet,[2] Book,[3] and Scroll.[4] [p. 34] If there be, above the pen that writes, something which constrains it to service, its type will be the Hand.[5] If the Presence which embraces Hand and Tablet, Pen and Book, is constituted according to a definite order, It will be typified by the Form or Image.[6] And if the human form has its definite order, after that likeness, then is it created "in the Image, the Form, of the Merciful One". Now there is a difference between saying, "In the image of the Merciful One," and, "In the image of Allâh." For it was the Divine Mercy that[7] caused the image of the Divine Presence to be in that "Image." And then Allâh, out of His grace and mercy, gave to Adam a summary "image" or "form," embracing every genus and species in the whole world, inasmuch that it was as if Adam were all that was in the world, or were the summarized copy of the world. And Adam's form--this summarized "image"--was inscribed in the handwriting of Allâh, so that Adam is the Divine handwriting, which is not the characters of letters (for His Handwriting transcends both characters and letters, even as His Word transcends sound and syllables, and His Pen transcends Reed and Steel, and His Hand transcends flesh and bone). Now, but for this mercy, every son of Adam would have been powerless to know his Sovereign-Lord; for "only he who knows himself knows his Lord." This, then, being an effect of the divine mercy, it was "in the image

---

[1] S. 68.
[2] S. 85, 22 and 7, 44.
[3] S. 2, 1.
[4] S. 25, 3,
[5] S. 48, 36.
[6] S. 82, 8; cf. 64, 3.
[7] There must, I think, be some corruption in the text here. I suggest reading ### for ###.]

of the Merciful One," not "in the image of Allâh," that Adam was created. So, then, the Presence of the Godhead is not the same as the Presence of The Merciful One, nor as the Presence of The Kingship, nor as the Presence of the Sovereign-Lordship; for which reason He commanded us to invoke the protection of all these Presences severally. "Say, I invoke the protection of the Lord of mankind, the King of mankind, the Deity of mankind! [1] If this idea did not underlie the expression [p. 35] "Allâh created man in the image of the Merciful," the words would be linguistically incorrect; they should then have run, "after His image."[2] But the words, according to Bokhari, run, "After the image of the Merciful."

But as the distinction between the Presence of the Kingship and the Presence of the Lordship call for a long expression, we must pass on, and be content with the foregoing specimen of the symbolic method. For indeed it is a shoreless sea.

But if you are conscious of a certain repulsion from this symbolism, you may comfort yourself by the text, "He sent down from heaven rain, and it flowed in the valleys, according to their capacity;[3] for the commentaries on this text tell us that the Water here is knowledge, and the Valleys are the hearts of men.

4. The Permanent Validity of the Outward and Visible Sign: an Example

Pray do not assume from this specimen of symbolism and its method that you have any licence from me to ignore the outward and, visible form, or to believe that it has been annulled; as though, for example, I had asserted that Moses had

---

[1] S. 114.]

[2] And so they are quoted on p. [7].

[3] S. 13, 19.]

not really shoes on, did not, really hear himself addressed by the words, "Put thy shoes from off thy feet."[1] God forbid!--The annulment of the outward and visible sign is the tenet of the Spiritualists (Bâṯiniyya), who, looked, utterly one-sidedly, at one world, the, Unseen, and were grossly ignorant of the balance that exists between it and the Seen. This aspect they wholly failed to understand. Similarly annulment of the inward and invisible meaning in the opinion of the Materialists. (Hasha-wiyya). In other words, whoever abstracts and isolates the outward from the whole is a Materialist, and whoever abstracts. the inward is a Spiritualist, while he who joins the two together is catholic, perfect. For this reason the Prophet said, "The Koran has an outward and an inward, an ending and a beginning" (a Tradition which is, however, possibly, traceable to 'Alî, as its pedigree stops short at his name). I assert, on the contrary, that 'Moses understood from the command "Put off thy shoes" the Doffing of the Two Worlds, and obeyed the command literally by putting off his two sandals, and spiritually by putting off the Two Worlds. Here you just have this cross-relation between the two, [p. 36] the crossing over from one to the other, from outward word to inward idea. The difference between the true and false positions may be thus illustrated. One man hears the word of the Prophet, "The angels of Allâh enter not a house wherein is a dog or a picture," and yet keeps a dog in the house, because, he says, "The outward sense is not what was meant; but the Prophet only meant, 'Turn the dog of Wrath out of the house of the Heart, because Wrath hinders the knowledge which comes from the Lights Angelical; for anger is the demon of the heart."' While the other first carries out the command literally; and then says, "Dog is not dog because of his visible form, but because of the inner idea of dog--ferocity, ravenous-ness. If my house, which is the abode of my person, of my body,

---

[1] S. 20, 12.]

must be kept clear of doggishness in concrete form, how much more must the house of my heart, which is the abode of man's true and proper essence, be kept clear of doggishness in spiritual idea!" The man, in fact, who combines the two things, he is the perfect man; which is what is meant when it is said, "The perfect man is the one who does not let the light of his knowledge quench the light of his reverence." In the same way he is never seen permitting himself to ignore one single ordinance of religion, for all the perfection of his spiritual Insight. Such a thing is grievous error; an example of which is the evil which befell some mystics, who called it lawful to put by literal prescriptions of the Shariat as you roll up and put-by a carpet; insomuch that one of them perhaps went so far as to give up the ordinance of prayer, saying, forsooth, that he was always at prayer in his heart! But this is different from the error of those fools of Antinomians (Ibâḥiyya) who trifle with sophisms, like the saying of one, "Allah has no need of our works"; or of another, "The heart is full of vices from which it cannot possibly be cleansed," [p. 37] and did not even desire to eradicate anger and lust, because he believes he is [not] (?) commanded to eradicate them. These last, verily, are the follies of fools; but, as for the first-named error, it reminds one of the stumble of a high-bred horse, the error of a mystic whom the devil has diverted from the way and "drawn him with delusion as with cords[1]

To return to our discussion of "the Putting-off of the Shoes." The outward word wakens one to the inward signification, the Putting-off of the Two Worlds. The outward symbol is a real thing, and its application to the inward meaning is a real truth. Every real thing has its corresponding real truth. Those who have realized this are the souls who have attained the degree of

---

[1] S. 7, 21

the Transparent Glass (we shall see the meaning of this presently). For the Imagination, which supplies, so to speak, the clay from which the symbol is formed, is hard and gross; it conceals the secret meanings; it is interposed between you and the unseen lights. But once let it be clarified, and it becomes like transparent glass, and no longer keeps out the light, but on the contrary becomes a light-conductor. nay, that which keeps that light from being put out. by gusts of wind. The story of the Transparent Glass, however, is coming; meanwhile, remember that the gross lower world of the imagination became to the Prophets of God like a transparent "glass" shade and "a niche for lights"; a strainer, filtering clear the divine secrets; a stepping-stone to the World Supernal. Whereby we may know that the visible symbol is real: and behind it lies a mystery. The same holds good with the symbols of "the Mountain," "the Fire," and the rest.

5. Another Example of this Two-sided and Equal Validity of Outward and Inward

When the Prophet said, "I saw Abdul-Rahmân enter Paradise crawling," you are not to suppose that he did not see him thus with his own eyes. No, awake he saw him, as a sleeper might see him in a dream, even though the person of Abdul-Rahmân b. `Awf was at the time asleep in his house. [p. 38] The only effect of sleep in this and similar visions is to suppress the authority of the senses over the soul, which is the inward light divine; for the senses preoccupy the soul, drag it back to the - Sense-world, and turn a man's face away from the world of the Invisible and of the Realm Supernal. But, with the suppression of sense, some of the lights prophetical may become clarified and prevail, inasmuch as the senses are no longer dragging the soul back to their own world, nor occupying their whole attention. And so it sees in waking what others see in sleep. But if it has attained absolute perfection, it is not limited to apprehending the visible form merely; it passes direct from that to the 'inner idea, and it is disclosed to such an one that faith is drawing the soul of an Abdul-Rahmân to the World Above (described by the word "Paradise", while wealth and riches are drawing it down to this present life, the World Below. If the influences which draw it to the preoccupations of this world are more stubborn than those which draw it to the other world, the soul is wholly turned away from its journey to Paradise. But if the attraction of faith is stronger, the soul is merely occasioned difficulty, or retarded, in its course, and the symbol for this in the world of sense is a crawl. It is thus that mysteries are shown forth from behind the crystal transparencies of the imagination. Nor is this limited to the Prophet's judgment about Abdul Rahmân only, though it was only him he saw at that time. He passess judgment therein on; every man whose spiritual vision is strong, whose faith is firm, but whose wealth has so much multiplied that it threatens to crowd out his faith, only failing to do so because the power of that faith more than counterbalances it. This example illustrates to you the way in which prophets used to see concrete objects, and have immediate vision of the spiritual, ideas behind them. Most frequently the idea, is presented to their direct inward vision first, and then looks down from thence on to [p. 39] the imaginative spirit and receives the imprint of some concrete object, analogous to the idea. What is conferred by inspiration in sleeping vision or dreams needs interpretation. [1]

(ii) THE PSYCHOLOGY OR THE HUMAN SOUL: ITS FIVE FACULTIES OR SPIRITS

---

[1] (Note by Ghazzâlî.) The proportion borne by dreams to the other characteristics of prophethood is as one to forty-six. That borne by waking vision has a greater ratio-as one to three, I believe, for it has been revealed to us that the prophetic characteristics fall definitely into three categories, and of these three one is waking vision.]

The gradations of human Spirits Luminous; in knowing which we may know the symbolism of the Light-Verse in Koran.

The first of these is the sensory spirit. This is the recipient of the information brought in by the senses; for it is the root and origin of 'the animal spirit, and constitutes the differentia, of the animal genus. It is sound in the infant at the breast.

The second is the imaginative spirit. This is the recorder of the information conveyed by the senses. It keeps that information filed and ready to hand, so as to present it to the intelligential spirit above it, when the information is called for. It is not found in the infant at the beginning of its evolution. This is why an infant wants to get hold of a thing when he sees it, while he forgets about it when it is out of his sight. No conflict of desire arises in his soul for something out of sight until he gets a little older, when he begins to cry for it and asks to have it, because its image is still with him, preserved in his imagination, This faculty is possessed by some, but not all animals. It is not found, for example, in the moth which perishes in the flame. [p. 40] The moth makes for the flame, because of its desire for the sunlight, and, thinking that the flame is a window opening to the sunlight, it hurries on to the flame, and injures itself. Yet, if it flies on into the dark, back it comes again, time after time. Now had it the mnemonic spirit, which gives permanence to the sensation of pain that is conveyed by the tactile sense, it would not return to the flame after being hurt once by it. On the other hand, the dog that has received one whipping runs away whenever it sees the stick again.

Third, the intelligential spirit. This apprehends ideas beyond the spheres of sense and imagination. It is the specifically human faculty. It is not found in the lower animals, nor yet in children. The objects of its apprehension are axioms of necessary and universal application, as we mentioned in the section in which the light of intelligence was given precedence over that of the eye.

Fourth, the discursive spirit. This takes the data of pure reason and combines them, arranges them as premises, and deduces from them informing knowledge. Then it takes, for example, two conclusions thus learned, combines them again, and learns a fresh conclusion; and so goes on multiplying itself ad infinitum.

Fifth, the transcendental prophetic spirit. This is the property of prophets and some saints. By it the unseen tables and statutes of the Law are revealed from the other world, together with several of the sciences of the Realms Celestial and Terrestrial, and pre-eminently theology, the science of Deity, which the intelligential and discursive spirit cannot compass. It is this that is alluded to in the text, "Thus did We inspire thee with a spirit from Our power. Thou didst not know what is the Book, nor what is Faith, [p. 41] but we made that spirit a light wherewith we guide whom We will of our vassals. And thou, verily, dost guide into a straight way."[1] And here, a word to thee, thou recluse in thy rational world of the intelligence! Why should it be impossible that beyond reason there should be a further plane, on which appear things which do not appear on the plane of the intelligence, just as it is possible for the intelligence itself to be a plane above the discriminating faculty and the senses; and for relations of wonders and marvels to be made to it that were beyond the reach of the senses and the discriminative faculty? Beware of making the ultimate perfection stop at thyself! Consider the intuitive faculty of poetry, if thou wilt have an example of everyday experience, taken from those special

---

[1] S. 42, 52

gifts which particularize some men. Behold how this gift, which is a sort of perceptive faculty, is the exclusive possession of some; while it is so completely denied to others that they cannot even distinguish the scansion of a typical measure from that of its several variations. Mark how extraordinary is this intuitive faculty in some others, insomuch that they produce music and melodies, and all the various grief-, delight-, slumber-, weeping-, madness-, murder-, and swoon-producing modes! Now these effects only occur strongly in one who has this original, intuitive sense. A person destitute of it hears the sounds just as much as the other, but the emotional effects are by him only very faintly experienced, and he exhibits surprise at those whom they send into raptures or swoons. And even were all the professors of music in the world to call a conference with a view of making him understand the meaning of this musical sense, they would be quite powerless to do so. Here, then, is an example taken from the gross phenomena which are easiest for you to understand. Apply this now to this peculiar prophetical sense. And strive earnestly to become one of those who experience mystically something [p. 42] of the prophetic spirit; for saints have a specially large portion thereof. If thou canst not compass this, then try, by the discipline of the syllogisms and analogies set forth or alluded to in a previous page, to be one of those 'who have knowledge of it scientifically. But if this, too, is beyond thy powers, then the least thou canst do is to become one of those who simply have faith in it ("Allâh exalts those that have faith among you, and those who acquire knowledge in their several ranks").[1] Scientific knowledge is above faith, and mystic experience is above knowledge. The province of mystic experience is feeling; of knowledge, ratiocination, and of faith, bare acceptance of the creed of one's fathers, together with an unsuspicious attitude towards the two superior classes.

---

[1] S. 58, 11

You now know the five human spirits. So we proceed: they are all of them Lights, for it is through their agency that every sort of existing thing is manifested, including objects of sense and imagination. For though it is true that the lower animals also perceive these said objects, mankind possesses a different, more refined, and higher species of those two faculties they having been created in man for a different, higher, and more noble end. In the lower animals they were only created as an instrument for acquiring food, and for subjecting them to mankind. But in mankind they were created to be a net to chase a noble quarry through all the present world; to wit, the first principles of the religious sciences. For example, a man may, in perceiving with his, visual sense a certain individual, apprehend, through his intelligence, a universal and absolute idea, as we saw in our example of Abdul Rahmân the son of `Awf.

PART III.--THE APPLICATION TO THE LIGHT-VERSE AND THE VEILS TRADITION

(i) THE EXPOSITION OF THE SYMBOLISM OF THE LIGHT-VERSE

WE now come to what the symbolism of this Verse actually signifies. The full exposition of the parallelism between these five classes of Spirit, and the fivefold Niche; Glass, Lamp, Tree, and Oil, [p. 43] could be indefinitely prolonged. But we must be content with shortly indicating the method of the symbolism.

1. Consider the sensory spirit. Its lights, you observe, come through several apertures, the eyes, ears, nostrils, etc. Now the aptest symbol for this, in our world of experience, is the Niche for a lamp in a wall.

2. Take next the imaginative spirit. It has three peculiarities: first, that it is of the stuff that this gross lower world is made of, for its objects have definite and limited size, and shape, and dimension, and are definitely related to the subject in respect of distance. Further, one of the properties of a gross substance whereof corporal attributes are predicated is to be opaque to the light of pure intelligence, which transcends these categories of direction, quantity, and distance. But, secondly, if that substance is clarified, refined, disciplined, and controlled, it attains to a correspondence with and a similarity to the ideas of the intelligence, and becomes transparent to light from them. Thirdly, the imagination is at first very much needed, in order that intelligential knowledge may be controlled by it, so that that knowledge be not disturbed, unsettled, and dissipated, and

so get out of hand. The images supplied by the imagination hold together the knowledge supplied by the intellect. Now, in the world of everyday experience the sole object in which you will find these three peculiarities, in relation to physical lights, is Glass. For glass also is originally an opaque substance, but is clarified and refined until it becomes transparent to the light of a lamp, which indeed it transmits unaltered. Again, glass keeps the lamp from being put out by a draught or violent jerking. [p. 44] By what, then, could possibly the imagination be more aptly symbolized?

3. The intelligential spirit, which gives cognizance of the divine ideas. The point of the symbolism must be obvious to you. You know it already from our preceding explanation of the doctrine that the prophets are a "Light-giving lamp."

4. The ratiocinative spirit. Its peculiarity is to begin from one proposition, then to branch out into two, which two become four and so on, until by this process of logical division they become very numerous. It leads, finally, to conclusions which in their turn become germs producing like conclusions, these latter being also susceptible of continuation, each with each. The symbol which our world yields for this is a Tree. And when further we consider that the fruit of the discursive reason is material for this multiplying, establishing, and fixing of all knowledge, it will naturally not be typified by trees like quince, apple, pomegranate, nor, in brief, by any other tree whatever, except the Olive. For the quintessence of the fruit of the olive is its oil, which is the material which feeds the lamps, and has this peculiarity, as against all other oils, that it increases radiance. Again, if people give the adjective "blessed" to specially fruitful trees, surely the tree the fruitfulness whereof is absolutely infinite should be named Blessed! Finally, if the ramifications of those pure, intellectual propositions do not admit of relation to

direction and to distance, then may the antitypical tree will be said to be "Neither from the East nor from the West."

5. The transcendental prophetic spirit, which is possessed by saints as well as prophets if it is absolutely luminous and clear. For the thought-spirit is divided [p. 45] into that which needs be instructed, advised, and supplied from without, if the acquisition of knowledge is to be continuous; while a portion of it is absolutely, clear, as though it were self-luminous, and had no external source of supply. Applying these, considerations, we see how justly this clear, strong natural faculty is described by the words, "Whose Oil were well-nigh luminant, though Fire touched it not;" for there be Saints whose light shines so bright that it is "well-nigh"' independent of that which Prophets supply, while there be Prophets whose light is "well-nigh" independent of that which Angels 'supply. Such is the symbolism, and aptly does zit typify this class.

And inasmuch as the lights of the human spirit are graded rank on rank, then that of Sense comes first, the foundation and preparation for the Imagination (for the latter can only be conceived as superimposed after Sense); those of the Intelligence and Discursive Reason come thereafter. All which explains why the Glass is, as it were, the place for the Lamp's immanence; and the Niche, for the Glass: that is to say, the Lamp is within the Glass, and the Glass within the Niche. Finally, the existence, as we have seen, of a graded succession of Lights explains the words of the text "Light upon Light."

Epilogue: the Darkness Verse

But this symbolism holds only for the 'hearts of true believers, or of prophets and saints, but not for the hearts of misbelievers; 'for the term "light" is expressive of right-guidance alone. But as for the man who is turned from the path of guidance, he is false, he is darkness; nay, he is darker than darkness. For darkness is natural; it leads one neither one way nor the other; but the minds of misbelievers, and the whole of their perceptions, are perverse, and support each other mutually in the actual deluding of their owners. They are like a man "in some fathomless sea, overwhelmed [p. 46] by billow topped by billow topped by cloud; darkness on darkness piled!"[1] Now that fathomless sea is the World, this world of mortal dangers, of evil chances, of blinding trouble. The first "billow" is the wave of lust, whereby souls acquire the bestial attributes,[2] and are occupied with sensual pleasures, and the satisfaction of worldly ambitions, so that "they eat and luxuriate like cattle. Hell shall be their place of entertainment!"[3] Well does this wave represent darkness, therefore; since love for the creature makes the soul both blind and deaf. The second "billow" is the wave of the ferocious attributes, which impel the soul to wrath, enmity, hatred, prejudice, envy, boastfulness, ostentation, pride. Well is this, too, the symbol of darkness, for wrath is the demon of man's intelligence; and well also is it the uppermost billow, for anger is mostly stronger even than Just; swelling wrath diverts the soul from lust and makes it oblivious of enjoyment; lust cannot for a moment stands up against anger at its height, Finally, "the cloud" is rank beliefs, and lying heresies, and corrupt imaginings, which become so many veils veiling the misbeliever from the true faith, from knowledge of the Real, and from illumination by the sunlight of the Koran and human intelligence. For it is the property of a cloud to veil the shining of the sunlight. Now these things, being all of them darkness, are well called "darkness on darkness piled", shutting the soul out from the knowledge of things near, [p. 47] let alone things

---

[1] S. 24, 40.
[2] The following tripartite division of the soul, with its analogues, is Platonic (see Republic, bk. iv).
[3] S. 12, 47.

far away; veiling the misbeliever, therefore, from the apprehension of the miraculousness of the Prophet, though he is so near to grasp, so manifest upon the least reflection. Truly it might be said of such an, one that "when a man putteth forth his hand, he can well-nigh see it not."[1] Finally, if all these Lights have, as we, saw, their source and origin in the great Primary, the One Real, then every Confessor of the Unity may well believe that "the man for whom Allâh doth not cause light, no light at all hath he."[2]

And now you must be content with thus much of the mysteries of this Verse.

(ii) THE EXPOSITION OF THE SYMBOLISM OF THE SEVENTY THOUSAND VEILS

What is the signification of the tradition, "Allâh hath Seventy Thousand Veils of Light and Darkness: were He to withdraw their curtain, then would the splendours of His Aspect surely consume everyone who apprehended Him with his sight." (Some read "seven hundred veils;" others, "seventy thousand.")

I explain it thus. Allâh is in, by, and for himself glorious. A veil is necessarily related to those from whom the glorious object is veiled. Now these among men are of three kinds, according as their veils are pure darkness; mixed darkness and light; or pure light.

The subdivisions of these three are very numerous. That much only is certain. I could no doubt make some far-fetched enumeration of these subdivisions; but I have no confidence in the results of such defining and enumerating, for none knows

---

[1] S. 24, 40.
[2] S. 24, 40.

whether they were really intended or not. As for the fixing of the number at seven hundred, or at seventy thousand, this is a matter that only the prophetic power can compass. My own clear impression, however, is that these numbers are not mentioned in the way of definite enumeration at all, for [p. 48] numbers are not infrequently mentioned without any intention of limitation, but rather to denote some indefinitely great quantity:--God knows best! That point, then, is beyond our competence, and all I can do now is to unfold to you these three main divisions and a few of the subdivisions.

1. Those veiled by Pure Darkness

The first division consists of those who are veiled by pure darkness. These are the atheists "who believe not in Allâh, nor the Last Day." [1] These are they "who love this present life more than that which is to come," [2] for they do not believe in that which is to come at all. They fall into subdivisions.

First, there are those who desire to discover a cause to account for the world, and make Nature that cause. But nature is an, attribute which inheres in material substances, and is immanent in them, and is moreover a, dark one, for it has no knowledge, nor perception, nor self-consciousness, nor consciousness, nor light perceived through the medium of physical sight.

Secondly, their are those whose preoccupation is self, and who in no wise busy themselves about the quest for causality. Rather, they live the life of the beasts of the field. This veil is, as it were, their self-centred ego, and, their lusts of darkness; for there is no darkness, so intense as slavery to self-impulse and

---

[1] S. 4, 37.
[2] S. 14, 3.

self-love. "Hast thou seen," saith Allâh, "the man who makes self-impulse his god?"[1] and the Prophet, "Self-impulse is the hatefullest of the gods, worshipped instead of Allâh."

This last division may farther be subdivided. There is one class which has thought that this world's Chief End is the satisfaction, of one's wants, lusts, and animal pleasures, whether connected with sex, or food, or drink, or raiment. These, therefore, are the creatures of pleasure; pleasure is their god, the goal of their ambition, and in winning her they believe that they have won felicity. Deliberately and willingly do they place themselves at the level of the beasts of the field; nay, at a viler level than the beasts. Can darkness be conceived more intense than this? Such men are, indeed, veiled by darkness unadulterated. Another class has thought that man's Chief End is conquest and domination--the taking of prisoners, and captives, and life. [49] Such is the idea of the Arabs, certain of the Kurds, and withal very numerous fools. Their veil is the dark veil of the ferocious attributes, because these dominate them, so that they deem the running down of their quarry the height of bliss. These, then, are content to occupy the level of beasts of prey, nay, one more degraded still. A third class has supposed that the Chief End is riches and prosperity, because wealth is the instrument for the satisfaction of every lust. Their concern is therefore the heaping up and multiplication of riches--the multiplication of property, real estate, personal estate, thoroughbreds, flocks, herds, fields and the rest. Such men hoard their pelf underground--you may see them toiling their lives long, embarking on perils by land, perils by sea, up-date, down-lea, piling up wealth, and yet grudging it to themselves--and how much more others! These are they whom the Prophet had in view when he said, "Poor wretch, the slave of money! Poor wretch, the slave of gold!" And, indeed, what darkness is in tenser than that which

---

[1] S. 25, 43.

blinds mankind to the fact that gold and silver are just two metals, unwanted for their own sakes, no better than gravel unless they are made a means to various ends, and spent upon things worth spending on? A fourth class had advanced a step higher than the total folly of these last, and has supposed that the supreme felicity is found in the extension of a man's personal reputation, the spread of his own renown, the increase of his own following and his influence over others. You may see these admiring themselves in their own looking-glasses! One of them, who may be suffering hunger and penury at home, will be spending his substance on clothes, and trying to look his smartest therein, [p. 50] just in order to avoid contemptuous glances when he walks abroad!

Innumerable are the varieties of this species, and one and all are veiled from Allâh by pure darkness, and they themselves are darkness. So there is no need to mention all the individual varieties, when once attention has been called to the species. One of these varieties which we should, however, mention is the sort that confesses with their tongues the Creed "There is no god but Allâh," but are probably urged thereto by fear alone, or the desire to beg from Mohammadans, or to curry favour with them, or to get financial assistance out of them, or by a merely fanatical zeal, to support the opinions of their fathers. For if the Creed fails to impel these to good works, by no means shall it secure their elevation from the dark sphere to light. Rather are their patron-saints devils, who lead them from the light into the darkness. But he whom the Creed so touches that his evil deeds displease him and his good deeds give him pleasure, has passed from pure darkness even though he be a great sinner still.

2. Those veiled by mixed Light and Darkness.

The second division consists of those who are veiled by mixed light and darkness. It consists of three main kinds: first, those whose darkness has its origin in the Senses; secondly, in the Imagination; thirdly, in false syllogisms of the Intelligence.

First, then, those veiled by the darkness of the Senses. These are persons who one and all have got beyond that self-absorption which was the characteristic of all the first division, as they deify something outside the self, and have some yearning for the knowledge of the Deity. The first grade of these consists of the idol-worshippers, the last grade consists of the dualists; between which extremes come other grades.

The first, the idolaters, are aware, in general, that they have a deity whom they must prefer to their dark selves, and believe [p. 51] that their deity is mightier than everything else, and more to be prized that every prize.

But the darkness of sense veils from them the knowledge that they must transcend the world of sense in this quest; so that they make for themselves from the more precious minerals, gold, silver, gems, etc., figures splendidly fashioned, and then take those images unto themselves as gods. Such men are veiled by the light of Majesty and Beauty from the attributes of Allah and his light: they have affixed these attributes to sense-perceived bodies; which sense has blocked out the light of Allah; for the senses are darkness in relation to the World Spiritual, as we have already shown.

The second class, composed of the remotest Turkish tribes, who have no organized religious community and no definite religious code, believe that they have a deity, and that that deity is some particularly beautiful object; so that when they see a human being of exceptional beauty, or similarly a tree, or a horse, etc., they worship it and call it their god. These are veiled by the light of Beauty mixed with the darkness of Sense. They have penetrated further than the idolaters into the Realm of Light in the discovery of Light, for they are worshippers of Beauty in the absolute, not in the individual; and they do not limit it specially to one individual to the exclusion of others; and then, again, the Beauty they worship is of Nature's hand, and not of their own.

The third class say, Our deity must be in His essence Light, glorious in His express image, majestic in Himself, terrible in His presence, intolerant of approach; and yet He must be likewise perceptible. For the imperceptible is meaningless in the opinion of these. Then because they find Fire thus characterized, they worship it and take it unto themselves as lord. Such are veiled by the light of Dominion and of Glory, [p. 52] which are, indeed, two of the Lights of Allah.

The fourth class think that, since we have control over fire, kindling or quenching it at will, it cannot serve as divinity. Only that which possessing the attribute of Dominion and Glory and has us under its absolute sway, and is withal very higher and lifted up-only this avails for divinity. Astrology is the science that is celebrated among this folk, the attribution to each star of its special influence: so that some worship Cynosura and others Jupiter, and others some other heavenly body, according to the many influences with which they believe the several stars are endued. These, then, are veiled by Light, the Light of the Sublime, the Luminous, the Potent; which are also three of the Lights of Allâh.

The fifth class support the fourth in their fundamental idea, but they say that it does not befit their Lord to be describable as small or great among light-giving substances, but He must be the greatest of them; and so they worship the Sun, which, they say, is the Greatest of All. Such are veiled by the Light of

Greatness, in addition to the former lights; but are still blent with the darkness of the Senses.

The sixth class advance higher still and say, The sun has no monopoly of light; bodies other than the sun have each one its light. So, as the deity must have no partner in lightfulness, they worship Absolute Light, which embraces all lights, and think that It is the Lord of the Universe, and that all good things are attributable to it. Then, since they perceive the existence of evils in the world, and will by no means allow them to be attributed to their deity, He being wholly void of evil, they conceive of a struggle between Him and the Darkness, [53] and these two are called by them, as I suppose, Yazdân and Ahriman; which is the sect of the Dualists.

This must suffice for the exemplification of this division, the classes whereof are more numerous than those we have mentioned.

Second, those veiled by some light, mixed with the darkness of the Imagination. These have got beyond the senses, for they assert the existence of something behind the objects of sense, but are unable to get beyond the imagination, and so have worshipped a Being who actually sits on a throne. The meanest grade of these is called the Corporealists; then all the various Karrâmites, into whose writings and opinions we cannot go here, for to multiply words thereon were bootless. But the highest in degree are those who denied to Allah corporality and all its accidentia, except one--direction, and that direction upwards; for (say they) that which is not referable to any direction, and cannot be characterized as either within or without the world, does not exist at all, since it cannot be imagined by the imagination.[1] They failed to perceive that the

---

[1] See Averroes, opusc. cit., p. 61, Cairo ed., p. 51

very first degree of the intelligibilia takes us clean beyond all reference whatsoever to direction and dimension.

Third, those who are veiled by Light divine, mixed with the darkness of false syllogisms of the Intelligence, and who worship a deity, that "Heareth, Seeth, and hath Knowledge, Power, Will, Life", and transcends all directions, including direction upwards; but whose conception of these attributes is relative to their own; so that some of them may even have declared outright that His "speech" is with sounds and letters like ours; while others advanced a step higher, it may be, and said, "Nay, but it is like our thought-speech, both soundless and letterless." Thus, when they were challenged to show that "hearing, sight, life", etc., are real in Allâh they fell back on what was essentially anthropomorphism, though they repudiated it[1] formally; for they utterly failed to apprehend what [p. 54] the attribution of these ideas to Allah really signifies. Thus they, say, in regard to His will, that it is contingent, like ours; that it is a demanding and a purposing, like ours. All of which opinions are well-known, and we need not go into further details with regard to them: These, then, are veiled by several of the divine Lights, mixed with the darkness of false syllogisms of the intelligence. All such are various classes of the second division, which consists of those veiled by mixed light and darkness.

3. Those veiled by Pure Light

The third division are those veiled with, pure Light, and they also fall into several classes. I cannot enumerate all, but only refer to three.

---

[1] It seems inevitable to read ###. The feminine Pronoun could only refer to ### which makes nonsense. To refer it to a supplied masdar does not seem to be in our author's manner.]

The first of these have searched out and understood the true meaning of the divine attributes, and have grasped that when thee divine attributes are named Speech, Will, Power, Knowledge, and the rest, it is not according to our human mode of nomenclature. And this has led them to avoid denoting Him, by these attributes altogether, and to denote Him simply by a reference to His creation, as 'Moses did in his answer to Pharaoh, when the latter asked, "And what, pray, is the Lord of the Universe?" and he replied, "'The Lord, Whose Holiness transcends even the ideas of these attributes,' He, the Mover and Orderer of the Heavens."[1]

The second mount higher than these, inasmuch as they perceived that the Heavens are a plurality, and that the mover of every several Heaven is another being, called an Angel, and that these angels form a plurality, and that their relation to the other Lights Divine is as the relation of the stars to[2] all other visible lights.[3] Then they perceived that these Heavens are enveloped by another Sphere, by whose motion all the rest revolve once in twenty-four hours, and that finally The LORD is He Who communicates motion to this outermost Sphere, which encloses all the rest, on the ground (say they) that plurality must be denied of Him.

The third mount higher than these also, [p. 55], and say that this direct communication of motion to the celestial bodies must be an act of service to the Lord of the Universe, an act of worship and obedience to His command, and rendered by one of His creatures, an Angel, who stands to the pure Light Divine in the relation of the Moon to the other visible lights; and they

---

[1] See S. 26, 23 ff..
[2] Reading ### for ###.
[3] Cf. S. 41, 11.]

asserted that the LORD is the Obeyed-One of this Angelic Movent, and that the Almighty must be considered the universal Movent indirectly and by way of command only (amr),[1] but not directly by way of act. The explication of which "command" and what it really is contains much that is obscure, and too difficult for most minds, besides being beyond the scope of this book.

These, then, are grades all of which are veiled by Lights without admixture of Darkness.

4. The Goal Of the Quest

But those who ATTAIN make a fourth grade, to Whom, in turn, it has been made clear that this Obeyed-One, if identified with, Allâh, would have been given attributes negative of His pure Unity and perfection, on account of a mystery which it is not in the scope of this book to reveal; and that the relation of this Obeyed-One to THE REAL EXISTENCE is as the relaxation of the Sun to Essential Light, or of the live coal to the Elemental Fire, and so "turned their faces"[2] from him who moves the heavens and him who issued the command (amara) for their moving, and Attained unto an Existent who transcends ALL that is comprehensible by human Sight or human Insight; for they found IT transcendent of and separate from every characterization that in the foregoing we have made.

And these last are also divided. For one class the whole content of the perceptible is consumed away--consumed, obliterated, and annihilated; yet the soul itself remains contemplating the absolute Beauty and Holiness and contemplating herself in her beauty, which is conferred on her by this Attainment unto the

---

[1] See S. 7, 53
[2] See M. pp. [30, 31]

Presence Divine [p. 56] In them, then, the seen things, but not the seeing, soul, are obliterated.

And they are passed by others, among whom are the Few of the Few; whom "the splendours of the Countenance sublime consume,"[1] and the majesty of the Divine Glory obliterate; so that they are themselves blotted out, annihilated. For self-contemplation there is no more found a place, because with the self they have no longer anything to do. Nothing remaineth any more save the One, the Real; and the import of His word, "All perisheth save His Countenance,"[2] becomes the experience of the soul. To this we have made reference in the first chapter, where we set forth in what sense they named this state "Identity," and how they conceived the same.

Such is the ultimate degree of those who Attain. Some of these souls had not, in their upward Progress and Ascent, to climb step by step the stages we have described; neither did their ascension cost them any length of time; but with their first flight they attained to the knowledge of the Holiness and the confession that His sovereignty transcends everything that it must be confessed to transcend. They were overcome at the very first by the knowledge which overcame the rest at the very last. The onset of God's epiphany came upon them with one rush, so that all that is apprehensible by the sight of Sense or by the insight of Intelligence was by "the splendours of His Countenance utterly consumed". It may be that that first was the way of Abraham, the Friend of Allâh, while the latter was the way of Mohammed, the Beloved of Allâh. Allâh alone knoweth the mysteries of their Progress and of their Stations on the Way of Light.

---

[1] See the Tradition on p. [2]
[2] S. 28, 88.

Such is our account of the classes of the veiled by the Veils; and it were not strange, if, after all these Stations were fully classified and the veils of the Pilgrims Mystical were fully studied, the number of classes were found to amount to Seventy Thousand. Yet, if you look carefully, you shall find that of them all not one falls outside the divisions which we have set forth. For, as we have shown, they must be veiled by their own human attributes or by the senses, imagination, discursive intelligence; or by pure light.

This is what has occurred to me by way of answer [57] to your interrogations, though, these came to me at a time when my thought was divided, and my mind preoccupied, and my attention given to other matters than this. May not my suggestion be, then, that you ask forgiveness for me for anything wherein my pen has erred, or my foot has slipped? For 'tis a, hazardous thing to plunge into the fathomless sea of the divine mysteries; and hard, hard it is to essay the discovery of the Lights Supernal that are beyond the Veil.

www.ingramcontent.com/pod-product-compliance
Lightning Source LLC
Chambersburg PA
CBHW051549010526
44118CB00022B/2635